# How to Buy
# the Right Shares
# at the Right Time

A simple step-by-step guide to buying
the best shares at the best time written
specifically for retail investors.

RICHARD MORGAN

ISBN: 1530359406
ISBN 13: 9781530359400

# Disclaimer and a Note to the Reader

This book is written and designed to provide accurate and authoritative information on the subject of stock picking and stock valuation. The contents of this book are intended as a general guide on the topics covered in it. If professional advice is needed, you should seek advice from qualified financial professionals about your individual financial plan and situation.

This book is sold with the understanding that neither the author nor the publisher is engaged in rendering legal, accounting, or other professional services by publishing this book. At the time of publishing, the author's professional qualifications to offer specific investment advice have lapsed; therefore, nothing in this book constitutes a recommendation to buy or sell shares in a specific company or sector. Investors must exercise their own judgement, which they should be able to do with the aid of this book, or alternatively seek professional guidance. At the time of publishing, the author does not hold shares in Marks & Spencer or Debenhams and has no immediate plans to do so.

As of the date of publishing, all the contents in the book, such as information, data, and web links, are up to date to the best knowledge of the author and publisher. The author and publisher cannot be held responsible for any inaccuracies.

The author and the publisher specifically deny responsibility for any liability, loss, or risk that may be suffered as a direct or indirect consequence of applying any of the ideas contained in this book.

# About the Author: Richard Morgan

Richard left university in 1996 with a degree in Geography and his first job was as a research assistant for David Evennett MP at the Houses of Parliament.

In 1997 he joined the back office of HSBC Investment bank, and he spent one year working his way towards the trading floor. In 1998 he moved into the front office of the investment bank and initially joined the futures and options desk, where he witnessed the bursting of the dotcom bubble and was a futures trader on September 11, 2001 (the infamous day of the attack on the Twin Towers in New York).

He moved on to the special-situations trading desk of HSBC, which specialized in mergers and takeovers of listed securities.

He remained at HSBC until 2005, when he joined ING Investment Bank again as a special-situations and M&A trader. During his time at the leading Dutch bank, Richard continued to trade and invest, witnessed the volatility related to the subprime debt bubble, and watched the demise of Lehman's and many other leading institutions.

In 2011 Richard left ING as he had a burning desire to start his own businesses. He is now a fully fledged retail investor and has to split his time between investing, running three small businesses, and spending time with his family and friends. He even coaches his son's football team. He knows all the pressures involved with being a retail investor and how real life gets in the way.

Richard is uniquely placed as a former market professional with a significant amount of professional trading history and experience, who is currently living the life of a retail investor. He is regarded as one of the best retail-investor trainers, having the ability to make very complex subjects sound basic and easy to understand.

In 2016 Richard took his knowledge of the stock market and of running a small business to create the Retail Investor Academy. This academy is specifically aimed at helping retail investors succeed in the stock market.

# About the Retail Investor Academy

The Retail Investor Academy was launched in 2016 and has the sole aim of helping retail investors learn the right information in the right way so they can become successful investors. This academy is specifically and exclusively aimed at retail investors, and everything is geared towards them.

The academy offers a range of material, from books (like this one) to DVD sets, webinars, seminars, and small monthly events. The academy also arranges a large-scale annual event each year with guest speakers, leading analysts, and company management, all aimed at helping retail investors succeed.

The academy also offers a monthly membership club, where members receive a monthly magazine packed with more information specifically relevant to retail investing. In addition to the magazine, members are invited to a one-hour webinar or seminar each month where the author of this book, Richard Morgan, will present and train members on another key aspect of retail investing.

The most popular product offered by the Retail Investor Academy is called "Ultimate Investing". This unique course is held only once a year, and consists of 10 live online sessions (one a week for ten weeks). By the end of "Ultimate Investing", you should have a good understanding of the markets and how to be a successful investor.

For more information about the academy, please visit www.retail-investor-academy.co.uk or e-mail hello@r-i-a.co.uk.

If you are interested in attending a seminar or one of our events or in joining our monthly membership club, we would be delighted to welcome you aboard. Everything the academy does is aimed at nonprofessional (or retail) investors, so it will be easy to follow and understand.

# To get us started…

A group of retail investors who were thirty years old decided to meet for lunch and discuss stocks and shares. They decided to meet at the Bull & Bear pub in Manchester because the pub was young, friendly, had great beer, and close to several nightclubs where they could go after their meeting and paint the town red.

Ten years later, when they were forty years old, the same retail investors decided to meet for lunch and discuss stocks and shares. They decided to meet at the Bull & Bear pub in Manchester because the pub had a lively, energetic vibe, but it was quiet enough so they could talk "without shouting," and the waitresses wore tight-fitting miniskirts and the waiters tight-fitting shirts.

Ten years later, when they were fifty years old, the same retail investors decided to meet for lunch and discuss stocks and shares. They decided to meet at the Bull & Bear pub in Manchester because there was good, professional service; good-quality food; a fantastic wine list; and a friendly atmosphere.

Ten years later, when they were sixty years old, the same retail investors decided to meet for lunch and discuss stocks and shares. They decided to meet at the Bull & Bear pub in Manchester because the food was good value and filling, so they could order a large steak and chips, and this could be their main meal of the day, and they would not need to eat dinner later that evening.

Ten years later, when they were seventy years old, the same retail investors decided to meet for lunch and discuss stocks and shares. They decided to meet at the Bull & Bear pub in Manchester because there was plenty of parking, it was a convenient location, the food was good quality and good value, and they would not be affected by rush-hour traffic on their way back home again.

Ten years later, when they were eighty years old, the same retail investors decided to meet for lunch and discuss stocks and shares. They decided to meet at the Bull & Bear pub in Manchester because there were disabled parking places; a disabled ramp to get in and out of the pub; a stair lift; and good, clean disabled toilets inside. The pub also did nice, light food like salads and sandwiches, so they would not get too bloated and would not need to eat dinner later that evening.

Ten years later, when they were ninety years old, the same retail investors decided to meet for lunch and discuss stocks and shares. They decided to meet at the Bull & Bear pub in Manchester because none of them had ever been there before!

Not really relevant, but I just thought it was funny!

# Contents

# Introduction

When I finished the first draft of this book, it totalled over sixty thousand words. I passed it around to friends and colleagues to see what they thought about it, and I asked for their honest opinions. The feedback I got was almost unanimous. It was too short and too simple to be a credible nonfiction book about the stock market. I took that feedback on board and went through the book again, simplifying it further and making it even shorter. I want this book to be different from a normal nonfiction book about stocks and shares!

The truth is, you can make investing in the stock market as easy or as difficult as you want to. Some of the simplest strategies make money, while some of the most complex don't. I will show you a very simple fifteen-step strategy to finding good shares, but most important is when you buy them! Timing is everything, which I will prove to you.

Investing should not be a roller coaster of action and emotion; it should actually be quite boring and mundane. It does not take long to research a stock and make a good judgement on whether you should buy it or not; however, the truth is that so few retail investors do any research at all. Some retail investors are willing to spend hours researching holiday flights to get the best deal, but on the other hand, they are willing to invest in shares of Thomas Cook Ltd with little more than a tip written on a website by somebody they have never met.

Finding good shares is pretty easy, and by the end of this book, you will have the knowledge to find them. For this reason, this book represents an exciting opportunity for retail investors like you. I am genuinely excited about the change it could make in your investing life. You have made the first crucial step towards a better financial future by getting your hands on this book and starting to read it. There isn't a more simplistic step-by-step guide to investing on the market.

But the choice is now yours. I don't know the exact statistic, but publishers widely acknowledge that the vast majority of nonfiction books are never read. Sometimes the first few chapters are read, but the actual book is rarely finished. You have the choice now. You can put this book down and think, "I will read that later," or you can plough through and get to the end. If you do finish and understand its contents, you will be in a far better place to make good investment decisions.

The most common issue I hear from the retail investors I meet is that they don't know how to value shares. They have no idea if the shares they are buying are undervalued or overvalued, and they have no idea how to get this information.

It's not for lack of trying. Many retail investors understand the importance of this essential pillar of knowledge, and many have bought books, attended seminars, and tried to get their heads around EV/EBITDA ratios and dividend yields. However, these methods of valuation are about as far away from the thrill of actively trading in stocks and shares as possible. Many retail investors just can't bring themselves to learn off by heart the dull mathematical formulas (you don't have to!) needed for modern stock-price valuation. Trust me; stock valuation is quick and easy. By the end of this book, you will be able to value a stock in a few minutes. The best thing is, all the complicated formulas are done for you and are available from your broker, newspapers, or websites.

There are two other reasons why life is so tough for retail investors. The first is that many books in the marketplace that claim to be for beginners are outpourings of knowledge so that authors can clear their minds of everything they know about the subject. In reality, retail investors don't need to know absolutely everything there is to know. They need the basics, and they need relevant, key information only. Having basic knowledge so you know what a good share is and what it's not, knowing when to buy shares, and having the discipline to cut losers and let winners win is enough to succeed. You can build in some astrophysics if you like, but you are just needlessly complicating things.

The second issue is that many retail investors plough through these books and learn how to calculate a price-earnings ratio, but their calculations are different from those of Reuters, Bloomberg, or other key financial-markets news. This leads to further disillusionment and frustration, and many retail investors give up and revert back to trading a good story without any in-depth knowledge of valuation.

This book is my attempt to equip the retail investors of the world with the information, knowledge, and know-how to value a company and decide if the current share price is cheap or undervalued or expensive or overvalued.

I promise now: no technical financial-markets terminology. I promise to explain each concept as quickly and simply as I can. I promise not to tell you things you don't need to know. I will make this process as simple and painless as I can.

I should, however, point out that this is a book for long-term value investors. That means I will show you how to look for, find, and analyse shares with a view of buying them and keeping them for a significant period of time (it could be weeks, months, or years). This is not a get-rich-quick book that will teach you how to watch charts and buy at resistance levels and sell at support levels eight or nine times each day.

I believe that the vast majority of retail investors are not full-time day traders. They fit their investing in around busy lives, with jobs and families and hobbies. I have written this book for such people.

I have two fundamental beliefs about the stock market that you need to understand.

1. For some shares I believe there are long periods of time where their share prices do not accurately reflect the actual value of the underlying business. You must remember that when you buy shares, you are buying shares in a business, with real people and real products, services, and assets. I will show you and prove to you that there are times when their share prices get moved around for reasons completely out of their control. A company that has nothing to do with the Internet can be valued higher than it should be during the dotcom boom, and the same company that has nothing to do with subprime lending can be valued lower than it should be during the banking crisis. The most recent example of this was BREXIT, with companies who export little to the EU taking a huge hit in the days following the referendum result. You must understand that the stock market moves around, driven by sentiment and can price individual stock illogically and irrationally! This is why buying shares at the right time is so important.

2. I also believe that fundamentals do eventually drive individual share prices. I believe the most important piece of fundamental data

is earnings (the amount of profit a company is making). It may take the stock market weeks, months, or years to realize, but the stock market will eventually reward companies with good fundamentals and good earnings. That's why buying the right shares is so important.

I believe that to buy the right shares, you are looking for

- companies with growing earnings or profits,

- companies without too much debt,

- companies that look undervalued and are performing well, and

- companies that have good management and a good story.

I believe that to buy at the right time, you are trying to

- buy shares at times the stock market in general is down and depressed,

- buy shares at times the stock has been forced lower than its fundamental value for reasons beyond its control against logic and common sense,

- sell shares at times the stock market in general is high and optimistic, and

- sell shares at times the stock has been forced higher than its fundamental value for reasons beyond its control.

So I believe that if you buy the right shares at the right time, the market will eventually offer you the right price for your shares. This could take weeks, months, or years, but I promise you that eventually it will happen.

There is one caveat to all this simplicity. We will still get things wrong! There will be times we think we are buying the right shares at the right time, but we made a mistake and got it wrong! That's fine; the very best investors get things wrong all the time, but we must trade out and take the loss. We must cut losing positions when we have made a mistake, and we must be in the mindset that we are happy to do so. The very best full-time fund managers, people who earn millions each year and have the full resources of research departments and cutting-edge financial data would be delighted if they got 70 percent of their trades right and made a 15percent return on their investments each year. Yet some retail investors take each loss personally, and many run their losing positions for years, waiting for the stock price to recover, not wanting to admit they made the wrong call. I am going to spend a lot of time and effort convincing you it's OK to make mistakes; you will get things wrong! If you are not getting anything wrong, you are not really trying! If you get more right than wrong, and cut your losers as soon as you realize it's the wrong share to own, and let your winners win, you will do just fine!

The first section of this book (phase 1) is all about quantitative data. This is just a fancy word for data that is based on facts and mathematics. We will look at a number of ratios that can help us understand the current performance of the company and where it sits in terms of current valuation. We will look at ratios that help us understand if a company is undervalued or overvalued, how much debt it has, what dividends it pays, how it's using its assets, and what its growth prospects are. This all sounds really scary, but trust me; it's not. These ratios are all around you, all the time. You don't need a degree in mathematics to calculate them; all the hard stuff is done for you. You just need to know where to find them and how to interpret them.

The second section of this book (phase 2) is all about qualitative data. This means stuff that's based more on opinion and interpretation than on fact—things like the story behind the company, its competitive strengths, and how good its managerial team is.

My ultimate measure of success is that any retail investor should be able to spend around five minutes looking at a share and its current market price and be able to make a rough "all things considered" estimate about the value of the company and a snap judgement about its current share price. This is what I call phase 1.

If you decide it's an interesting company that you want to research further, you then move on to phase 2, which is all about researching the company and building an investment case around it. I think this two-phase approach will dramatically improve the success rate of retail investors, while also saving them a significant amount of time and effort researching companies that are dead ends.

I am not hoping anybody who reads this book will be in a position to get a full-time job as a company analyst at a leading investment bank.

This brings me to my first warning. This book is written for retail investors. I make absolutely no apology for this. If you are a professional investor, you may find my simplification of this issue crude. You may feel the need to contact me and tell me that I have oversimplified complicated company valuations. Feel free to e-mail me at spam@retail-investor-academy.com and tell me all your concerns, but please don't expect any response.

For the Benjamin Graham purists out there, I know I don't go into enough depth. Please don't feel the need to contact me and tell me. For the Warren Buffet fans, I know and understand that you feel you can't value a company without an in-depth analysis of its break-up value and calculation of the sum of its parts. However, I am making an assumption that average retail investors do not have teams of twenty top accountants sitting in their living rooms, willing to conduct long-term investigations into core company values.

I have devised a simple, fifteen-step process that retail investors will be able to understand and follow. If you are thinking of investing in a stock, you will be able to apply my fifteen-step process and get a rough guide of the valuation of that share. Once you have this knowledge, you will be better equipped to make investment decisions.

I believe in value investing but not in its purest form. I believe that retail investors need to invest on the same principles as value investors, but retail investors have to cut corners, take shortcuts, and look for advantages wherever they can. This book is a list of those shortcuts. It is an attempt to level the playing field between retail investors and professional investors. It teaches retail investors how to think and invest like professionals while not doing the same amount of work the professionals do.

Retail investors need to understand they have some advantages over the professionals. Professional investors need to invest at all times, even at times they don't want to or during periods where they don't understand what's going on in the markets. Retail investors don't have to invest during these periods; we can sit and watch and wait for market conditions we are happy with.

Professionals live and breathe the market; they are too close and live through every second of peak and trough. Every day they think about stocks and shares and nothing else! I remember when I was working at HSBC during a five-day losing streak for the markets; the professionals were losing money, everybody was down and depressed, and it felt like Armageddon was consuming us all. It was impossible not to let that environment impact on your thinking. I needed the afternoon off to attend my uncle's funeral and was amazed how nobody in the outside world cared a jot about what was happening to the stock market. Life was happening as normal, completely unaware of the five-day losing streak.

When I returned to my desk after the funeral, I was amazed how I was back into the all-encompassing doom and depression of stocks and shares. As non-professional investors, we can distance ourselves and not get caught up in the market frenzy of boom and bust! We can see the wood from the trees during times the market is rising or falling. Retail investors have more perspective on life in general; we won't get flustered and think the world is ending just because a set of economic data is marginally lower than forecast. This should allow us to sit back and pick off the professionals when the market is too low or too high!

You should also realize that professional investors have to pick a strategy and stick to it, so long only investors have to buy and hold shares even when the market is falling. We don't have to. We can switch our strategy around to suit the current environment. Retail investors have advantages over the professionals. We can choose the battlefields we want to fight on at our time of choosing; the professionals don't have this luxury! Yes, they have the systems, the accountants, the analysts, and the knowledge, but that still does not stop them from getting things wrong!

I just want to emphasise this point again! I can significantly move the goalposts so the investment world is more in your favour, but we will still get things wrong. Professional investors can get a team of ten clever analysts in a room and spend weeks researching a specific company and still get it wrong. On this basis, what hope do we have? As retail investors, we will get stuff wrong, and acknowledging this is a cornerstone of this book. I believe that by following the fifteen steps in this book, you will get more right than you will get wrong (a 60 percent success rate is perfect; anything higher is amazing). However, you must be disciplined, admit when you get it wrong, and cut those losers.

This book will only work if you accept that you will lose money on some trades and that you will have to cut them. In general, retail investors hate losing money and hate cutting losing positions, but you have to! Don't take a loss as a personal insult. It is part of investing, and every professional investor accepts this as part of the job. As a retail investor, if you can embrace losing money when you have picked a loser but have the self-discipline to let your winners (the ones you get right) win, this book and that temperament can secure your financial future.

I have to be honest; there is a whole other set of pillars that retail investors need to know and understand to be successful. They include the importance of self-discipline, market psychology, economic releases that drive market sentiment, technical analysis, the unique identity of each sector and each index, and many more. I have tried to cover as much general information as possible. However, the most difficult skill for a retail investor to master is basic fundamental analysis and valuation, and that's why this book tackles that subject head-on.

Once you know how to find undervalued shares and how to research investments properly, you will suddenly find a thirst for knowledge and will go looking for how to do the other stuff. I have no doubt about this.

So let's go back to the choice you now have in front of you. This book is in your hands, and all you have to do is read it. At the end of the first phase, you will be able to look at financial data and make a snapshot judgement about the company, its current position, and its current share price. It will take you around five minutes to decide if you like the look of the company or not. If you like it, move on to phase 2 and start building the background of the company and decide if you want to invest or not. I have made the financial-ratios section of this book as simple and painless as possible. I also stress that you don't really need to learn the ratios or memorize how to calculate them; you just need to know what they are, how to interpret them, and where to find them!

If you fight your way through and get to step 9, you will be able to pick any share in the world, look at its key facts, and make a snapshot decision about its value and whether it's a worthwhile investment or not in a few minutes. The best thing is that once you have this skill, you will have it for the rest of your life. I learned about EPS (earnings per share) and P/E (price-to-earnings) ratios about twenty years ago, and I still use them today on each and every share I look at. In twenty years' time, we will all still be looking at EPS and P/E, so you are about to learn a lifelong skill. A few hours of boredom now can change the financial direction of your life. Also remember, I have made this as fun and painless as I can.

Throughout this book I have used two real companies, Debenhams and Marks & Spencer, to give real-life examples of real companies. Please do not interpret this as a recommendation to buy these companies. They are just examples. I wanted to choose examples that everybody would know and could walk into one of their shops at any time to understand the business we are talking about.

I have also taken all the financial details and ratios which are free and widely available. If you go to any

| Debenhams Key Numbers | | | |
|---|---|---|---|
| Latest Share Price (P) | 76.73 | Net Gearing % | 58.65 |
| Market Capitalisation (m) | 944.85 | Gross Gearing % | 60.18 |
| Shares in issue (m) | 1227.08 | Debt Ratio | 41.03 |
| P/E Ratio | 10.13 | Debt-to-Equity Ratio | 0.46 |
| Total dividends per share (p) | 3.4 | Assets / Equity Ratio | 2.51 |
| Dividend Yield (%) | 4.42 | Cash / Equity Ratio | 3.83 |
| Dividend Cover (x) | 2.28 | Price to book value | 1.11 |
| NAV per share (p) | 0 | ROCE | 7.84 |
| Earnings per share (p) | 7.6 | EPS Growth (%) | 7.04 |
| 52 week high / low | 96.35 / 63.75 | DPS Growth (%) | 0 |

| Marks & Spencer Key Numbers | | | |
|---|---|---|---|
| Latest Share Price (P) | 409.45 | Net Gearing % | 58.46 |
| Market Capitalisation (m) | 6764.47 | Gross Gearing % | 60.97 |
| Shares in issue (m) | 1648.26 | Debt Ratio | 47.43 |
| P/E Ratio | 13.82 | Debt-to-Equity Ratio | 0.58 |
| Total dividends per share (p) | 18.00 | Assets / Equity Ratio | 2.56 |
| Dividend Yield (%) | 3.45 | Cash / Equity Ratio | 6.44 |
| Dividend Cover (x) | 1.97 | Price to book value | 2.66 |
| NAV per share (p) | 0.00 | ROCE | 9.86 |
| Earnings per share (p) | 29.5 | EPS Growth (%) | -8.62 |
| 52 week high / low | 600.00 / 694.60 | DPS Growth (%) | 5.88 |

free share price website you will probably see a table like the ones below.

If you have no idea how to interpret the above information, you should be excited! By the end of step 9, you will know what each and every item is and how to interpret them, and you will be able to make a snap judgement on investing or not.

Exciting times are just around the corner, so let's stop waffling and get on with it!

# PHASE 1

# Step 1:

# Where to Find the Right Shares

The first thing we need to do is find a company that we can research and possibly buy its shares. This brings me to an elephant in the room. I don't want to start this book by being negative or by making a sweeping generalization about retail investors, but I am going to anyway.

If you are a retail investor who is inexperienced at investing or trading, the worst possible place you can look for share tips or information is from other retail investors who are inexperienced at investing or trading. This may sound brutal, but we need to have an open and upfront conversation if we are going to become better investors.

To put it bluntly, if you don't know what you're doing, don't ask the opinion of other people who don't know what they're doing. You will reinforce each other's bad habits, and you will both make the same mistakes.

So in the first paragraph of step 1, I have ruled out dodgy share tips from your best mate, your local pub landlord, your taxi driver, and all those dodgy bulletin boards on share-investing websites. You need to find your own shares to invest in, and I will show you how below, but the first question you need to answer is what type of investments are you are looking for.

## What type of shares (investments) are you looking for?

Think of shares as people, not as things. Take your street where you live, for example. In the closest twenty houses to your house, some of your neighbours will be old and grumpy, some will be young and grumpy, some will be happy, some will have kids who leave their bikes on their drive, some will be good at gardening, and some will be good at DIY. It's a mixture of different people, at different stages of their lives, with different problems and different ambitions and plans. Some will earn more money than others; some will have more debt than others. Some have good prospects, and some don't.

This is exactly the same with shares. Some companies are old, steady, and reliable and not very exciting. They were exciting when they were young, but now they have grown up and are old and boring. Some shares are young and vibrant, even reckless with their own health and well-being. Some shares are fun and happy and excited about the future; some shares have been bruised and battered by life and can't get excited about their own prospects and are waiting for an inevitable retirement home.

So if you are going to buy one of these shares that have their own personalities, you need to think about what type of investment you want. If you are looking to invest a significant amount of money in something safe and solid to make extra income, you are probably looking at large cap (big market caps) with a high dividend yield. (Don't worry; we have a whole section on market caps, dividends, and yields coming up.)

However, if you are looking for fast capital gains, you probably want to invest in high-growth stocks. If you want penny shares with fast capital gains, you are probably a small-cap, high-growth investor.

Going back to the analogy about your street and your neighbours, if you wanted a young, fun New Year's Eve party for an exciting and uplifting start to the year, would you only invite your old, grumpy, and unfriendly neighbours who would complain about the loud music and lousy food?

If you don't know what I am talking about at this stage, don't worry. By the end of this book, you'll know exactly what I mean. However, you need to have a rough idea of the type of investment you want before you start looking for shares to buy. It's your decision if you want to invest in established blue-chip FTSE 100 companies or a young, small, and risky tech company. There is no right or wrong answer to this, and it will probably depend on your stage of life, dependents, savings, and so on. You may decide to invest 80 percent of your money in safe and steady investments and 20 percent in risky investments.

Again, it's totally up to you what type of investor you want to be, but you need to understand the concept that each share has its own history, life, and personality and will act differently under pressure. If you don't like the way it will react, don't buy it!

> ### Tip: Never invest money you can't lose
>
> If you need the money you are investing to pay your mortgage or school fees, or worse still, you need the profits you are going to make, this is a recipe for disaster.
>
> To be a good investor, you need to be detached and emotionless and have lots of self-discipline. If you need the money you are investing, you will not be able to cut your losers and move on without any baggage, and you won't be able to let your winners win.

### The lazy "follow a pro" share-selection process

If you ask me where I get 90 percent of my shares

from, I will tell anybody who'll listen that it's from following professional investors and getting them to do the majority of the work for me. I rarely invest in something unless I see the market professionals do it first.

I don't just do this for shares; I do this in life as well. For example, I needed a van for the other businesses I own and run, and one of the largest van auctions in the United Kingdom is close to where I live. Every Thursday morning, one can buy a van from around two hundred vans that are auctioned at significant discounts compared to buying them from garages or directly from "the trade."

I always buy our company vans from these auctions, but the problem I have is that I am not mechanically minded, and I have no idea what I'm looking for. I know to look for dents, chips on the windscreen, and tread on the tyres, but that's about it. However, at the auction, there are a number of trade buyers who do know what they're doing, and they do know what to look for.

Last year, I was at the auction, and I saw a van I wanted to buy. It had only done fifty thousand miles (nothing for a van; they can do three hundred thousand miles easy!), and I decided I would pay up to £5,000 for it. However, when the van entered the auction room, I noticed that none of the trade buyers were interested in it. The auctioneer started the bidding. "Can I have four thousand pounds? Anybody? Four thousand pounds."

There was silence.

"Thirty-eight hundred pounds. Anybody? Thirty-eight hundred pounds."

Still nobody. The van eventually sold for around £3,500, but none of the trade buyers were interested.

Think about this. I was willing to pay £5,000 for a van I thought was OK, but I didn't bid for it at £3,500. I was put off because the guys who know what they're doing were not interested. They come week in and week out and know what to look for, and if they were not interested in that van, they must have seen something I am not trained to see.

To this day, I have no idea what was wrong with it. It could have been fine, but I always look to see what the trained professionals are doing and factor that in before I take the plunge. For your information, I bought a similar but different van a few weeks later for £4,700, and I took comfort in beating two or three trained trade buyers to get it.

Some people reading this will think I'm mad, but it's just the way I roll. Sure, I may have missed out on an absolute bargain, but realistically, the professionals would not watch while a van was sold at completely the wrong price, so I don't lose any sleep at night.

I use the same thought process when I go looking for shares, and it's really easy to do. In the stock market, there are hundreds of professional investors who run funds of all shapes and descriptions. It's fiercely competitive as they search for retail and institutional investors to invest money in their funds. If you have a pension, you already have money invested in these types of funds.

There are literally hundreds of funds in the United Kingdom, ranging from equities (shares) to bonds, derivatives, and cash. There are funds that invest in high-growth shares, funds that invest in high-income shares, funds that invest in risky emerging markets and risky small-cap stocks, funds that invest in safe blue-chip companies, or funds that track the Financial Times Stock Exchange 100 Index (FTSE 100) or any other major index you can name. You can even invest in funds that specialize in tech stocks.

Name any type of stock you want to invest in, and there will be twenty or thirty funds to choose from.

Now the best thing is that if you identify the type of fund you are interested in, that fund will nearly always have a website where they list their top-ten positions (the top-ten stocks that they own). Better still, there are loads of general websites like Morningstar.com that list available funds, and on each page, they list the top-five positions held by that fund. This particular website even tells you if it's a new position or if they are adding to their position or reducing it.

Let me just clarify this. If you want to invest in a small-cap, high-growth stock, just go to a website where you can compare funds, search for all the "small-cap, high-growth funds," and start looking at what positions they hold.

You'll still need to do your own research and make up your own mind, because professional investors get things wrong (they actually get a lot wrong). But as a starting point, would you rather research a stock brought to your attention by a professional investor who has done a load of research, probably met with the company's management, and decided to buy shares in the company totalling 4, 5, or 6 percent of the fund's total net worth; or would you rather take the word of somebody you have never met on a random website bulletin board?

You'll want to sit up and take notice when it's a new position. A fund may have been sitting on an old position for four or five years and may be thinking of selling, so don't automatically assume you should buy the same shares it holds. However, if it's a new position and the fund matches your investment criteria, it's definitely worth researching.

Follow fund managers you like

It's also worth keeping a list of fund managers you like. All fund managers compete against each other, and their stats are available for everybody to see. Highlight a few you like, and keep in touch with what they are doing.

Also, when funds ask for more money from investors, the fund managers often give interviews on CNBC, Bloomberg TV, or other share-related magazines or websites. They will often be open and honest about what types of investments they look for and what shares they are interested in. If you think particular fund managers talk sense and seem to know what they are doing (remember that you can check their records), keep an eye on their funds and what their top-ten positions are, and watch for any further interviews or news stories about them.

I always watch an interview with fund managers. It's interesting to hear what they have to say about the world of stocks and shares, and I often get share tips.

**Stock screening**

This is my second-favourite way to find stocks. Some of the better financial websites have a stock-screener tool. If you don't know about this tool, go and play with one. They are amazing. Google Finance and the Telegraph website offer stock-screening tools (https://www.google.co.uk/finance#stock-screener and http://shares.telegraph.co.uk/stock-screener). But there are many others to choose from. Just about any decent financial website will have a stock-screening tool.

The Internet has made this tool possible, and it's a real help for the retail investor. At this point, you may not know how to use them, but by the end of this book, you will.

Stock-screening tools allow you to screen stocks based on your investment priorities. For example, if you only want to invest in stocks with a market cap of £1 billion or more, a PE of 15 or lower, and a dividend yield of 5 percent or higher, you put these preferences into the stock screener. It will list every stock that meets those three criteria.

Again, I ask you, why would you listen to dodgy share tips on a message board when you can sort every listed share in the United Kingdom (and internationally as well) in a few seconds to fit the exact profile you are interested in? Obviously you still need to do further research, but what a great way to find shares!

## Look around you

Retail investors can also look for shares all around them, all the time. Companies' profits and share prices reflect real life and what's happening in the real world. If you come across a business that's rapidly expanding, look to see if it's listed on the stock exchange. If you see an amazing new product, look at who owns it and whether there are listed shares.

There is evidence all around you all the time. At the moment, it's hard to drive around the countryside in England without seeing building site after building site of new houses. It's no surprise that house-builder shares are currently performing really well. I am old now and not up with the latest technology, but when my friends all started using WhatsApp instead of Facebook, I jumped straight online to see who owned the company (FYI, Facebook bought WhatsApp in 2014; my friends were too late to help with this one!). The next time you are told about a great website or a fantastic new shop, look into the company and see if it has listed shares.

You are surrounded by information and clues that could take years to reach the clever analyst bod who lives and works in the cocoon of central London and who has never travelled north of the Watford Gap.

You can't just buy shares on the back of what you like and what you don't like, but it is reason enough to research the company.

A word of warning. You need to work out how big the company is and whether the new product or service will really make much difference. For example, if you regularly buy medication from a pharmacy, you may notice a new company that provides the drugs you take. If it's a small company, this could be a major game changer and worth researching. However, if the company is huge, the new drug may only account for a few percentage points in sales, and so it won't really make a difference.

**Tip:** Only invest in companies when you understand what they do, and you understand their business model. So many retail investors are happy to sink money into stocks when they have no comprehension of what the company does.

If you understand the company and understand what it does, you will be able to research it easier and also apply basic knowledge to your investment. For example, if you buy an airline stock, you can understand rising fuel prices or higher airline taxes hitting profits. However, if you buy a drug company that specializes in peptide therapeutics, you won't be able to get a really good understanding of the business and how the company is performing (unless you have medical training or work in that sector).

Stick to what you know, and play in stocks in

sectors you are good at. Investing is already difficult enough as it is. Don't penalize yourself by buying shares in companies that you have no idea about.

## Other places to find shares

Keep an eye on TV shows, newspapers, and magazines to see what they are writing or talking about. For example, if you are a keen gardener and often read gardening magazines, there could be an article talking about the future of genetically modified food that mentions a company doing groundbreaking research and developing an amazing new product. If you come across an article like this, go and research the company they are writing about!

It's also worth keeping an eye on the biggest winners and losers of each trading day. Almost all financial websites will tell you what the biggest individual gainers were, and it's worth jotting them down and putting them on your "research to-do" list. It's really interesting when the general stock market is going down but an individual stock is rising strongly for no specific reason—take a look at it!

## Key points from step 1

- Understand that each share has its own life, personality, history, and identity; just like a human, it will react differently under stress.

- Decide what type of investor you are. Are you safe and steady, looking for low-risk investments; or are you at high risk, looking for large and quick returns on your investment, happy in the knowledge that you could make large and quick losses?

- Once you know what type of investment you are looking for, find professional funds that share the same strategy and look at their top-ten holdings.

- Track and follow leading fund managers who share your investing philosophy.

- Use stock-screening tools to find interesting stocks.

- Look around you at the businesses and companies you use or can see doing well. If all your friends and family suddenly rush out and buy the latest gadget, service, or product, research the company behind it.

- Only invest in companies you can understand.

- Keep an eye on TV shows, magazines, and newspapers, and investigate if they start talking about an interesting business or stock.

- Keep an eye on the biggest winners and losers each day. If the market is down, but one particular stock has gone up on no direct news, research it!

As I said, I get 90 percent of my share tips from watching the positions of funds with a similar investment strategy to mine or watching or reading interviews with fund managers I like.

That's not to say that I just follow the crowd and do what the professionals do. I use them as filters to provide decent hints and tips of where to look. Professional fund managers get things wrong (everybody does), so I always make my own decisions and do my own research. However, I am a retail investor, and I don't have loads of time to research dead ends, so I use what the professionals are doing as a starting point.

Now that we have found a company we are interested in, it's time to start the research. For the sake of simplicity, let's assume you are interested in buying shares in Debenhams (the UK department store). Let's crack on and learn about step 2 and try to understand if Debenhams is a good buy or not.

# Step 2: Gather Key Information

As they said in *The Sound of Music*, let's start at the very beginning, a very good place to start.

So you're thinking about buying a share. Great. That's a good start. At this point, I'm not going to worry about where you have got this idea from. Even if you got it from a share-tipping service or bulletin board (please reread step 1 if you are still listening to dodgy share tips or reading dodgy bulletin boards), at least we have something to work with.

But where and how on earth do we start? We know at the end of step 1, you were hypothetically interested in buying shares in Debenhams, but how do we even begin to build the framework around this idea to try to understand if you are buying something that is under- or overvalued.

Let's just start at the beginning. Get a blank piece of A4 paper, and write down the name of the share you are thinking of buying. As soon as you do, we're off and running.

### Current share price

The current price of a share does not actually tell you a lot. It tells you nothing about the worth or value of the company you are buying. All it tells you is what people are currently willing to pay for a share.

As Warren Buffett said in one of his famous letters to his shareholders, "Price is what you pay, value is what you get."

You can't really tell if a share is expensive or cheap by looking at its share price alone. A share that trades at five pence can look really cheap in comparison to a share that trades at fifty pounds; however, it depends on the underlying value of the business. You could be getting better value paying fifty pounds a share for a great company than paying five pence a share for a terrible one.

Some retail investors seem to get their heads turned by penny shares. They look so cheap and enticing, and you can buy loads of them. Just because a share price looks cheap, that doesn't mean it can't get cheaper. Also, whether you invest £1,000 in shares worth five pence or five pounds, if the company goes bust, you have still lost 100 percent of your investment. Buying a mediocre company because its share price is cheap is a recipe for failure. You will lose money! Can I be any clearer?

> **Tip:** Just because a company is doing badly does not mean it can't do even worse!

Just looking at the current share price does not actually tell us much; however, let's make a note of it and move on.

### Shares within sectors? What are you talking about?

OK, that was easy. Next we need to work out what sector this share is in. The market is split into sectors so that similar types of stocks can be grouped together. For example, banks like Barclays, HSBC, and Lloyds will be in the (you guessed it) banking sector. Companies like Tesco and Sainsbury's are classified in the food-and-drug-retailers sector, but Debenhams and Marks & Spencer are classified as general retailers and so are in a different sector.

In step 1, I asked you to think about individual shares as being individual people. So think that each share has its own personality, history, future, prospects, and so on. Think about sectors as different parts of the country. For example, you have inner-city London that's full, busy, and buzzing with life, with theatres, bars, restaurants, nightclubs, and lots of other interesting stuff going on. You also have the suburbs of London, which are busy with lots of people and facilities, but life in the suburbs is gentler and more relaxed. Then you have areas of the country like the Cotswolds, where the pace of life is slow and pressure-free and all about calming green fields and blue skies (once or twice a year).

Each sector of the stock market has its own identity like the country. For example, if it's Saturday night and you are young and vibrant and you want to go to a techno-rave nightclub, you probably would not head for the peaceful Cotswolds (FYI, I am getting so old I don't know if a techno-rave nightclub is a real thing or not). Alternatively, if you are looking for a country pub complete with log fire and surrounded by countryside, you would probably not head to the suburbs of London.

Understanding and distinguishing the sector you are investing in is crucial. If you are looking for fast-paced action, you will be disappointed if you buy shares in a mature, slow, and steady sector and vice versa.

The utilities sector, for example (water, electricity, etc.), could be described as slow, methodical, even boring by some investors. Other investors will find the regular dividend payments and lack of news "surprises" as being very attractive. In comparison, the tech sector (Google, Amazon, etc.) could be described as fast, unpredictable, and exciting. This will appeal to some investors, and terrify others.

You must also remember sectors change over time; water and electric companies were once considered new and exciting, but many years later the sector has matured and got old and boring. A few years back, TVs and aeroplanes were the new exciting kids on the block. It's inevitable that one day, Internet stocks will be considered as old, boring, and conservative. You must know the identity and character of the sector you are investing in; otherwise you will not get the type of investment you are looking for.

Once you have worked out what sector your share is in and how you can expect the sector to act and perform, also write down all of its direct competitors. Make sure you make a note of only its direct competitors and not everything that is in the same sector. For example, betting companies like Ladbrokes or William Hill are placed in the leisure sector, but so is Domino's Pizza. There are not a lot of similarities between a betting company and a pizza company. You are looking for similar companies and the direct competitors.

For the point of this book, we are going to research Debenhams, and we are going to pick Marks & Spencer as its competitor. Ideally, you would choose three or four competitors in that same sector, but just by choosing two stocks, you will get the gist of what we are trying to do.

There are hundreds of places on the Internet where you can find information about sectors and what share is in each. I would be surprised if your broker's trading system (the parts you have access to) does not have some way of separating stocks by sector. However, if you are really struggling, please visit the financial section of the Telegraph website at www.shares.telegraph.co.uk/sectors for a good, basic list of stocks in each sector.

Once you have a list of all the competitors' stocks in the sector, you need to understand the size of your company versus all of its competitors. The easiest way to do this is by finding each company's market capitalization (oh no, our first real piece of financial jargon).

> **Tip:** As you get better at investing, you need to learn that each sector of the market has its own identity and way of trading. For example, mining stocks are heavily linked to commodity prices (the price of oil, copper, etc.), and professional investors realize that their share prices and earnings move in cycles.
>
> However, the utility-providers sector (electricity or water) is considered mature and stable, and investors often buy shares for their dividends and don't expect dramatic price rises.
>
> Each sector has its own unique identity and way of trading. If you understand the sector that your share is in, it will help you understand how the share will move and perform, and you won't get any nasty surprises.

## What is market capitalization?

Market capitalization (referred to as market cap) is the way to look at how big a company is.

The size of a company can also affect the way it can move and perform when placed under pressure. As a general rule, large companies change in small moves, and small companies change in large moves. For example, if a company makes a mistake and loses £25 million, this won't really matter if the company is huge and makes £500 million a year profits; it's a "drop in the ocean." However, if a small company that makes £50 million a year loses 50 percent of its profit losing the same £25 million, this is a huge change in their fortunes and will change their share price significantly.

If you want safe and steady investments that don't

move around much, don't buy small companies!

Working out a company's market capitalization is easy. It's the number of shares that have been issued by a company multiplied by the company's current share price. For example, if a company has issued five million shares and the current share price is two pounds per share, then the market cap of the company would be £10 million.

£2 × 5,000,000 shares = market cap of £10 million

So large companies are often called "large cap," which means they have a large market capitalization. I probably don't need to tell you, but smaller companies will be referred to as "small cap," meaning small market capitalization. I am not going to bother to tell you that "medium cap" companies have a medium market capitalization, because I sure you get it by now.

So find out all the market caps for your stock and its direct competitors. Once you have a list of the most relevant market caps, write down the current share prices of the stocks as well.

You now have the basics to compare different companies in the same sector by size and price. For example, your piece of paper may look something like this:

|  | Current Share Price | Market Cap |
|---|---|---|
| Debenhams | 76.73p | £944m |
| Marks & Spencer | 409.45p | £6.7bn |

The above table doesn't tell us that much at all. Marks & Spencer is the biggest company on our list and has the higher share price. Does that mean Debenhams is the best value, and we should all rush out and buy it? Absolutely not! Just wait a little longer, and we will gather some more information.

## Share liquidity or share volume

Have you ever wanted to buy something, and it's not available? Trying to buy Christmas decorations from my local Tesco in March is nearly impossible. When I complained to the store manager, she told me it's all to do with "supply and demand," apparently. You may decide to buy a new car, only for the car dealership to tell you it's not available in racing green until early next year. Houses are the worst — whenever you decide to move, there is never the right house available at the right price for you to buy!

Shares have the same problem and have supply-and-demand issues. Some larger shares have no problems at all with availability, but sometimes smaller shares can be like trying to buy Easter eggs in October (I complained to the same manager and got the same answer, FYI).

For this reason, you need to understand on average, how many shares a day does your stock trade? If you are looking at FTSE 100 companies, they will trade many millions of shares each day, and they will be considered very "liquid." However, if there is not much interest in your share and it only trades ten thousand shares a day, then this is considered very "illiquid."

You need to think about price as well. If the stock trades ten thousand shares, but the share price is seventy-five pounds per share, that's actually OK, because £750,000 worth of shares are traded each day. However, if the share price is five pence per share, than ten thousand shares is only £500 each day.

You have to be careful to look at the size of your company and how liquid the shares are before you buy them. Just about every share-quoting website has a volume section that tells you how many shares have traded and, on average, how many shares trade each day.

As a rule, I won't invest in anything that trades less than an average of £1,000,000 of volume each day. I prefer a higher turnover of shares, but £1,000,000 volume each day means I will probably be able to trade out of a position on short notice.

You should also understand how the share is traded. Most liquid stocks are traded via a supply-and-demand market book. Basically, this means that each person who is willing to buy a share puts a bid into the system, and each person who is willing to sell a share puts an offer in the system, and the computer matches them up where possible. This is a good, fair system, and investors normally get the right price.

Be warned that with illiquid shares, there are not enough people putting bids and offers in, so these shares have "market makers." A market maker is a trader who works for a bank, who always guarantees that the share has a bid and an offer price (this guarantees liquidity). In some ways, this is a great service because it means you can always trade an illiquid stock, but it also means you are trading with a market maker who may have an ulterior motive. Market makers may hold too many shares and want to sell them, or they may not have enough shares and want to buy some, so they can move the share price around and manipulate investors to get their own way.

You need to know whether your share is order-book traded or market-maker traded. If it's market-maker traded, you need to take into account that one or two people are setting the share price, and the share price may not react to fundamental news in the way you would expect. Also, if you put stop-loss levels in place and the market makers want to buy shares, don't be surprised if they drop the share price for a few hours, force you to sell, and then lift the price back up again.

There are some investors who won't buy shares in a stock that's run by market makers. This is a little extreme, but I can understand their opinion. I am happy to invest in stocks run by market makers, but I give them extra room to play around with share prices, and I don't get overly concerned with minor share-price moves.

> **Tip:** Always keep an eye on the link between share-price moves and volume. If a share price suddenly jumps or falls on small volume, be suspicious and don't read too much into the price moves. They could be caused by a market maker or one single aggressive buyer or seller.
>
> However, if the share price is moving, and it's backed up by a significant increase in trading volume, that means the share-price move is a lot more substantial, and something is going on. Sit up and take notice. Find out what's happening to your share! Volume is a real indicator of real news and fundamental change rather than just a trader or market maker playing around with the price.

### Fifty-two-week share-price range

This does exactly what it says on the tin: it tells you the highest and lowest price the stock has traded at in the last fifty-two weeks. As a stand-alone piece of information, this is pretty worthless, as we have no idea of the conditions or reasons why the stock traded so high or so low on those specific days. However, let's just take this opportunity to stop and think about this piece of data for a minute or two.

At the time of writing this book, the fifty-two-week range for Marks & Spencer was 391p (March 2016) to 600p (June 2015). That means in June 2015 the actual business behind the share price was valued at £9.9 billion. However, in March 2016, the value of the business was £6.4 billion. This means at some point between June and March, the business of Marks & Spencer must have lost £3.5 billion of value (approximately 35 percent), if it was trading at the right value at those times.

Let's look at Debenhams. At the time of writing this book, the fifty-two-week range was 64p (January 2016) to 97p (May 2015). This means the underlying business in May 2015 was worth £1.2 billion, but by January 2016 the real business (the actual shops, assets, etc.) was only worth £781 million. Again, in just a few months, there has been a monumental swing (approximately 36 percent) in the value of this business!

In reality, we all know that the real (actual) businesses behind Marks & Spencer and Debenhams (the real people, real food and clothes, real stores, and real assets) did not fluctuate by these extremes of value over such a short period of time. Maybe there were two or three stores that started making a loss, maybe a new clothing range went wrong, but nothing to wipe out £3.5 billion and £420 million, respectively. So what explains the massive swings in value of these two established and stable businesses?

You may be thinking I have taken two extreme examples to illustrate my point, but I have done precisely the opposite. Marks & Spencer and Debenhams are two of the most unexciting and conventional businesses I could find.

I challenge you to look at the fifty-two-week high and low prices for any stock you want, in any sector you want, at any time you want, and there will be a significant difference between the high and low prices. When you calculate the effect that the price move has had on the underlying value of the company, you realize how totally unreasonable the stock market can be when valuing constant, repetitive, and established companies that are just going about their day-to-day business.

This is a key point, and you need to understand that there is often a short-term disconnect between the share price of a company and the actual company itself. A company's share price can be lifted higher or lower in the short term from where the fundamental value of the company suggests it should trade. That's why timing is so important! This whole book is about trying to find the best shares to invest in but also the right time to buy them!

At this point I should introduce you to a chap called Benjamin Graham who wrote the first significant book about "value investing" in 1949, which was called *The Intelligent Investor*. In the book, Graham styled a fictional character called "Mr. Market." Graham described Mr. Market as a person you can trade with every day (Monday to Friday), who will always offer you prices on stocks, and you can decide if you want to buy, sell, or do nothing.

The problem is Mr. Market is a rampant schizophrenic and has a range of personalities. Some days he is happy, and nothing can upset him; on these days, he offers high prices, which you should sell at. On other days, he is a manic depressive and feels everything is terrible; on these days he offers low prices, which you should buy at. On other days, he is rational and offers fair prices.

Benjamin Graham's book and the concept of Mr. Market have become a mainstay and the lifeblood of value investors' theory and practice since 1949. You may think Mr. Market is unrealistic and far fetched, but it seemed a pretty accurate description of what was happening during the dotcom boom and bust and during the subprime banking crisis where stocks like Marks & Spencer traded as low as 210p (value £3.4 billion) and Debenhams traded at 23p (value £280 million).

Let's look how Marks & Spencer (a company with minimal exposure to Europe) traded following BREXIT. On June 23, 2016, Marks closed at 366p per share. The day after the vote (June 24, 2016), Marks opened at 276p per share, then fell to 255p per share, and rose to 340p per share before closing the day at 326p per share. Is that rational? Are the market professionals behaving in a calm, rational manner, or are they acting like a "rampant schizophrenic"?

The professional investors who manage our pensions and who earn millions each year in bonuses, wiped billions off the value of Marks and Spencer, only to add them back on again a few hours later. Again, I emphasize, Marks has minimal exposure to Europe. That day, the "real life" underlying true value of Marks barely changed, yet you could have invested in a company valued at £5.5bn at the twenty-four-hour high, or a company valued at £4.1bn at the twenty-four-hour low.

Market psychology is important to understand, and as retail investors, we should have enough distance and perspective to see the professionals losing their heads and take advantage when they do. Just think of it as shooting fish in a barrel!

Benjamin Graham's general philosophy, tools, and principles are as relevant today as they were in 1949, but we are retail investors in 2017, and we can't analyse stocks in the same way as he did in a post–World War II and Great Depression environment. In 2017 as retail investors, we may use different techniques to find and value shares we want to own, but we absolutely still need to buy into and adopt his notion about market psychology.

Market psychology is a whole different subject and

could be a book on its own, but you need to understand the following three principles so we can move forward.

1. The market can be irrational and in the short term can ignore the fundamental value of a company when determining its price. For example, larger stocks in the FTSE 100 Index can be more susceptible to FTSE-Index moves than to stock-specific news.

2. The market will eventually reflect a share at the right price (its real value), but this may or may not take a long time, so you need to decide if you can wait and roll with the punches while Mr. Market is having his violent mood swings.

3. Timing is everything. Think about your entry level when you buy a share (see step 14). You will probably make more money from an average share you buy at the right time and a low price, than from a good share you buy at the wrong time and a high price. Remember, the person who discovered electricity a few weeks after Benjamin Franklin had really bad timing!

## Competitive advantage and pricing power

You should also analyse if the company has a competitive advantage or not. Does the company have assets, infrastructure, or customers that its competitors can't reach? Can the company charge premium prices and still grow sales?

If the company you are looking at is an also-ran in its sector, seriously consider not investing.

You want to find companies that are market leaders or have a competitive advantage over everybody else. Look at electric cars, for example. Electric cars are widely considered the future, and it's assumed we will all be driving them by 2030 or 2040. If you believe electric cars are the future, you may want to invest in a company making them. You don't have a huge choice at the moment; the market leaders are companies like Tesla in the United States, who are all over electric cars and have been for some time.

Tesla have first-mover advantage; they have the brand recognition, brand desire, etc. At the time of writing this book (June 2016), they are still the only major car manufacturer to embrace electric cars and this inevitable future market. Soon all the other car manufacturers will start building electric cars; some will do it very well, but most of the others will just be "also ran's" in the sector. The key thing is that if other companies start to make slightly better and slightly cheaper cars than Tesla, they will still struggle to compete as Tesla already has the competitive advantage, brand desirability, and pricing power. Tesla are not home and dry. They still need to perform and make great cars to remain in pole position, but the ball is in their court.

Apple is another example we could look at in some detail. Apple have the brand recognition and have created a desire for their products unmatched in their sector. There are numerous mobile phone companies in China, possible making better, cheaper, more reliable, and stronger phones than the Apple iPhone, but they don't have the brand recognition or the pricing power so will always be playing catch up to Apple. As long as Apple don't upset its loyal supporters, which also happen to be its customers, it will be tremendously hard for any new company to knock them off their perch.

If you can find good-value companies that have a competitive advantage or pricing-power advantage in their sector, you should definitely investigate further.

## Does it have a relationship with its index?

If you asked me when I was eighteen years old what my life would be like, I don't think I would have ever predicted I would write a book with such a vague and random subheading as "Does it have a relationship with its index?" Life is funny, but hey-hoe, let's get on with it.

Some shares are "highly correlated" with their index. For example, the larger FTSE 100 companies are very closely linked to the FTSE 100 Index. This means that when the FTSE 100 Index goes up, they will go up as well, and vice versa. This is not just a general vague theory I have; it's because of a number of technical reasons, and here are just two of them.

1.  In essence, people who trade the FTSE 100 futures or options are basically trading a "basket" of one hundred stocks, so every time somebody buys or sells a future, all stocks in the FTSE 100 are bought or sold. FYI, the FTSE 100 future easily trades £1billion a day on a quiet day, so that's a lot of technical buying-and-selling pressure on FTSE 100 companies.

2.  There are hundreds of index-tracker funds out there that track the FTSE 100 Index. They create buying-and-selling pressure on FTSE 100 constituents just by tracking the index.

So as you can see, there are technical reasons why when the market goes up or down, all correlated stocks will go up or down with it. This is why during the dotcom boom, so many companies that had nothing to do with the Internet also got dragged higher and traded well above their fundamental valuations.

Going back to our BREXIT story about how Marks & Spencer traded on the day after the referendum vote — Marks was a victim of being highly correlated to the FTSE 100. The professionals were not specifically trading Marks that day. The company was being dragged along as there was huge speculation over the UK economy as a whole, and trading in the FTSE Futures and Options was huge. This is why Marks share price was so volatile on 24 June 2016, not because the professionals really felt the referendum vote was going to significantly impact that individual company; it was a general market thing.

So you may be thinking at this point that all you need to do is wait for the next time the FTSE 100 Index trades below four thousand points and buy any old FTSE 100 company, and you will make money. Well, to be fair, 99 percent of the time, you will. Some people will be banging this book at this stage and will be shouting, "It's not this easy," but it really is. Remember how I said in the introduction that investing is as easy or as complicated as you want to make it? Well, it's true.

If you have the patience to wait for years until the FTSE gets back below four thousand, just buy a collection of stocks that are highly correlated to the FTSE 100 Index, and by the time the FTSE 100 Index is trading back at five or six thousand points, you will be sitting on great profit on most if not all of them. If you follow steps 1 to 15 of this book and buy the best-value shares at this time, you will make even more money! Especially if you sell your highly correlated shares when the market gets back above seven thousand, which is the exact point most new retail investors are joining the party and deciding to buy shares for the first time.

Smaller shares will not be correlated with the FTSE 100 or FTSE 250 Index, and for these shares, fundamental analysis is crucial. These stocks will be driven by earnings and debt and dividends and all the things we are going to be talking about for the rest of this book. When the market is falling and all the large, traditional blue-chip companies are getting dragged lower alongside the market, these smaller stocks can be a safe haven for your money.

## Is Turnover Growing?

All businesses make money by selling their products, goods and services to their customers. This can be called sales, or revenue, or turnover but it's essentially the same thing, and principally means "how much stuff are they selling to their customers".

Ideally you want to see that a company is selling more and more each year. If its sales or revenue is stable, or falling, you are potentially entering a dangerous world.

Most decent stocks & share websites have a financials section, and revenue (or sales) is always in a fairly prominent position. All you need to do is find this financial section, locate the turnover (or revenue or sales) line, and jot down the last two or three years figures. The turnover number will almost always be at the top of the financials section. If you can't find it, don't worry it will be in the company's annual report which we will talk about in step 10. Better still, most websites will allow you to see a turnover chart, meaning you can go back years and years!

So for Marks & Spencer for example, turnover in 2013 was £10.027 Billion, in 2014 turnover was £10.310 Billion, in 2015 turnover was 10.331 Billion, and in 2016 turnover was 10.555 Billion. You can see this business is growing, but it's slow and steady. You could argue that Marks & Spencer is starting to stagnate in terms of growth, especially in comparison to the 2005 to

2012 period where the company was posting healthy year on year increases in turnover.

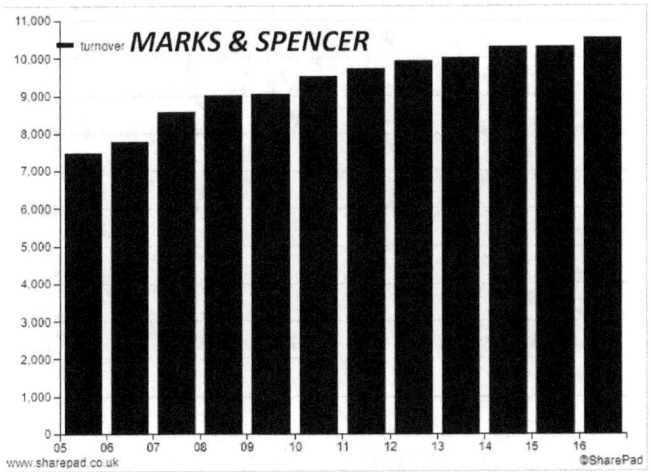

Debenhams turnover in 2013 was £2.282 Billion, in 2014 turnover was £2.313 Billion, in 2015 turnover was 2.323 Billion, and in 2016 turnover was 2.342 Billion. Again we are witnessing slow and steady growth, but again it's nothing like the good growth the company experienced during the 2005 to 2010 period.

If we were seeing falls in year on year turnover, this would be a red flag and would need further investigation. Maybe you could put the fall in turnover down to the fact that the company had restructured, or had sold part of its business, or maybe it's just a bad company experiencing problems.

However both Debenhams and Marks and Spencer are still growing year on year so we have something to work with, but we currently have concerns because the growth has slowed down from a sprint, to a jog, to a walk and is now at a plod.

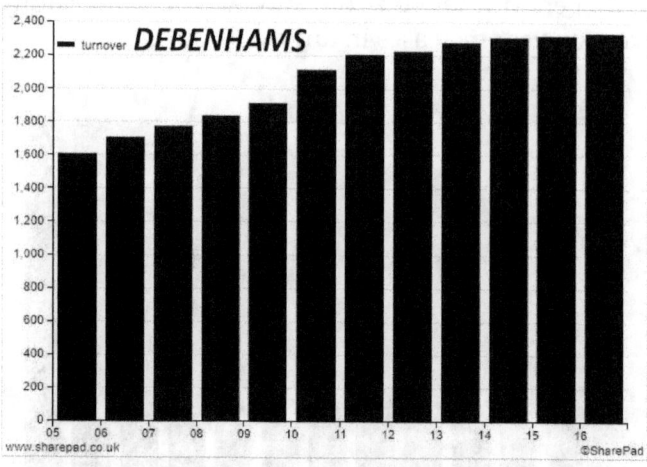

**TIP:** When looking at things like turnover growth, it's always a good idea to convert the numbers into percentage form. You do this by taking this years number and dividing it by last years number, subtracting one and multiplying by 100.

For example, 2016 Marks & Spencer turnover grew by just over 1% from 2015 turnover. Debenhams turnover also grew by just over 1%, which considering it's a much smaller company demonstrates that Marks & Spencer has the stronger overall growth out of the two companies!

We are looking for companies that are growing year on year, but you must have heard the saying "turnover is vanity, profit is sanity, cash is a reality"?

This is absolutely true for all businesses, including those listed on the stock exchange because a company may be growing but it's still a poor investment if it's not making any money (or profits). Even if it's making profits, is it able to convert these profits into cold hard cash? Our next step is to look at how to understand if a company is profitable or not. It's no good having a huge turnover if the business is not making any profit!

## Key points from step 2

- The current price of a share tells you its price, not the value of the company.

- Just because a share price has fallen a lot and is currently very low, that does not automatically mean you should buy it. Companies that perform badly can still perform even worse!

- Find out what sector your stock trades in, and create a list of its immediate competitors.

- Find out the personality, character, and temperament of the sector your stock trades in. Is the sector all about high growth and volatility, or is the sector mellow, mature, and relaxed?

- Find the market cap of your stock.

- Find out how liquid your stock is.

- Remember Mr. Market and try to understand what mood the market is currently in.

- Remember that stock prices can move aggressively over short periods of time. This does not mean the underlying value of the same company has moved much in this same time period. The timing of when you buy shares is crucial, and you need to buy when values of companies are lowest.

- Try to find a company with a competitive advantage and pricing power.

- Understand whether the share is a major constituent of its index, and if it is, be prepared to trade around the movements of that index.

- Understand if the business is growing, look at turnover and make sure you are seeing a year on year increase in sales growth.

So we have selected a share and got to know it a little bit better. We know what sector it's in, and we have some competitors to analyse the stock against. We have decided that its market cap is big enough to keep us interested, and it's liquid enough for us to trade in and out of. We have established that the company is growing each year.

However, we need lots more information. We need to know which competitor makes the most profit, has the least debt, and so forth. We need to know which has the best growth prospects and best management and so on. We are not ready to invest just yet, so let's move on to step 3.

# Step 3:

# Earnings per Share (EPS) and Price–Earnings (P/E) Ratios

So we are starting to get a little more detailed and technical now. Nothing to worry about, but I just want to remind you of some points I made in the introduction. I believe that the stock market eventually comes down to earnings (profits). It may take a long time, but the stock market will eventually reward a company that makes reliable, consistent profits with a higher share price. As long as we bought the shares at the right time, it's at this point we will make money! This is a fundamental belief of mine, so we need to find a few ways to analyse earnings (profits). I would like to start with a great ratio, EPS, or earnings per share.

You may be thinking, "Oh heck, here we go. We've only just started, and we're already into the financial ratios and boring stuff like EPS. This is the point where my eyes glaze over, and I put the book down and never pick it up again. I am going off to daydream about ice cream."

Please stick with me here. EPS is such a simple concept, and this small ratio can give you and all retail investors an instant view about a company and its fundamental value. It's as easy to find as a share price but far more revealing.

Let me put it a different way and ask you a question. If you have two companies, both of which make £100 million profit a year, which one do you buy? Come on, clever clogs, which company offers the investor better value? Company A, which makes £100 million profit each year, or company B, which also makes £100 million profit each year?

The answer is obvious. We don't know. We don't have enough information! Both companies make £100 million profit, but are they both the same?

Let me give you a bit more information, and let's see if you change your mind.

Company A has a market cap of £10 million and makes £100 million profit a year.

Company B has a market cap of £75 million and makes £100 million profit a year.

With just this tiny piece of information, we can suddenly look at this potential investment in a whole new light. Company A is quite small (£10 million market cap), yet it is making an amazing £100 million profit a year.

By comparison, Company B is quite large (£75 million market cap) and, by comparison, is making a disappointing £100 million profit each year.

This is what the EPS ratio does. It allows you to take an instant look, a snapshot, at a company and quickly work out how profitable it is in comparison to its size.

This is a great leveller for stocks. This allows you to compare the value of a company with five years' history and one hundred staff to a company with fifty years' history and ten thousand staff.

Let me give you another simple example.

Company A makes £100 million in profit each year.

Company B makes £250 million in profit each year.

With just this information, most people would buy shares in Company B, as it makes more profit.

However, suppose I were to tell you the following:

Company A has a market cap of £10 million and makes £100 million profit each year.

Company B has a market cap of £500 million and makes £250 million profit each year.

You can now see that although Company B makes more profit, Company A is significantly more profitable, so Company A is probably the more investable. (If you are thinking, "Yes, but it depends on what price you have to pay for a share in company A or B," you are right, but you will have to wait for a few minutes and the wonderful world of P/E ratios).

So what is an EPS ratio? It's simply an earnings-per-share calculation. Take the earnings of a company after tax (or profits of the company after tax), and divide it by the number of shares that have been issued.

You don't actually need to know how to calculate EPS. It's a widely used ratio across the financial markets, and companies often spend a lot of time and effort calculating their own EPS and publishing it in their accounts.

However, just so you can do it, if you ever need to, let's look at the calculation.

$$\frac{\textit{Earnings (or Company Profits after tax)}}{\textit{Number of shares in issue}} = EPS$$

So let's put some numbers against the calculation.

Company A has profits of £10 million a year and one hundred million outstanding shares in issue.

$$\frac{\textit{£10,000,000 Profit after tax}}{\textit{100,000,000 Outstanding Shares}} = 0.10x\ EPS$$

So Company A has an EPS of 0.10, or ten pence per share.

How do we use this newfound knowledge? Now that we know the EPS is 0.10 or ten pence, how does this help us?

We need to look at two things to start understanding value: the company's historical EPS and the comparison of our company's EPS versus its direct competitors in the same sector.

**Next we need to look at historic EPS**

The above company's EPS this year was ten pence per share. If it was nine pence last year and eight pence the year before, then the company is experiencing growth. This gives us a basic indication that everything is moving in the right direction. However, if the EPS is falling, this may (or may not) be a warning sign that something is going wrong. It should certainly create doubts about buying the shares until you have done some further investigation.

Comparing the EPS against other companies in the same sector is also crucial. This will give you a guide about how the sector as a whole is valued and how overvalued or undervalued your share is against its competitors.

### Debenhams versus Marks & Spencer

Take your piece of paper from step 1 and add EPS to it. It may start to look a little something like this:

|  | Current Price | Market Cap | EPS |
|---|---|---|---|
| Debenhams | 76.73p | £945m | 7.6p |
| Marks & Spencer | 409.45p | £6.8bn | 29.50p |

However, if you look at historic EPS, you will see Debenhams had 9.8p EPS in 2012, falling to 9.2p in 2013, falling to 7.1p in 2014, rising to 7.6p in 2015, and is currently to 7.6p this year. This is hardly the solid and consistent EPS growth we are looking for!

Marks & Spencer is not much better when looking at historic EPS. They posted 28.2p in 2013, rising to 32.2p in 2014, and then falling to 29.5p in 2015. Again like Debenhams, we are hardly pulling up trees, and we are not seeing regular, consistent year-on-year EPS growth.

Now we are getting a more informed opinion. Remember that Marks & Spencer has 1.6 billion shares issued, and Debenhams has 1.2 billion shares issued, yet Marks & Spencer has a vastly superior earnings-per-share ratio. Now we can start to understand why you would pay so much more for a Marks & Spencer share than a Debenhams share.

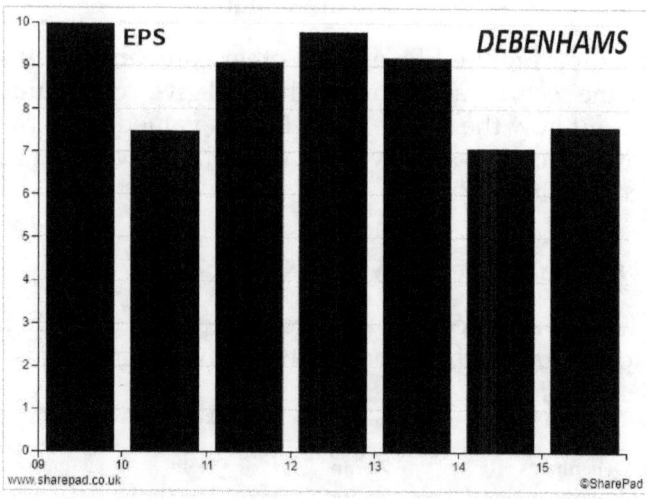

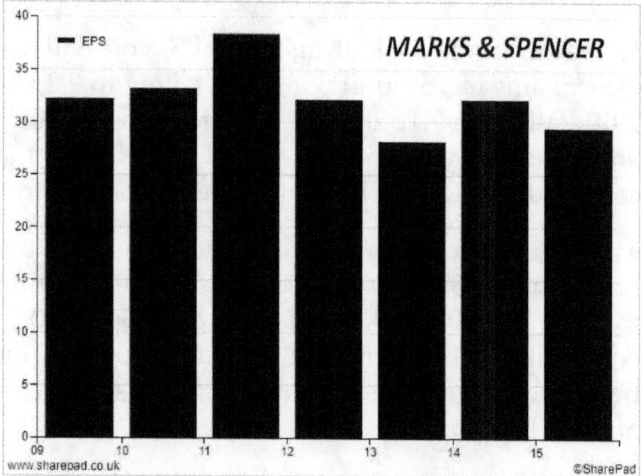

**Tip:** You must look for year-to-year earnings growth. This goes back to knowing your sector. Some new sectors, like technology, are all about fast growth, and some mature sectors, like utilities, are more about steady growth and dividend payments. However, you really want to invest in companies that have year-on-year (even quarter-by-quarter) earnings growth. Your tech company may be growing fast, and your utility company may be growing slow, but you want to see growth of some description.

If you buy a company where earnings are falling year on year, you could be on a rocky road to the town of Lossville.

I know what you're thinking: we need more information. We'll look at more ratios and formulas to help us, but we need to spend a little bit more time on EPS.

If you want to work out EPS for yourself, it's pretty easy to do. Just go to the earnings section for the last set of full-year company reports (wait for step 10; I will talk lots about company reports) and divide the earnings-after-tax figure by the number of outstanding shares, which you will normally find on the company website or on any financial website that deals with stock prices.

However, the EPS of a company is available in a number of places without having to work it out yourself. On just about every website that gives you details about stocks and stock prices, there will be a section that gives you an EPS calculation as well as the current stock price. Go and look, and you will find EPS calculations everywhere.

The issue is that the EPS is often different, depending on the website you are looking at. This often leads retail investors to pull their hair out. There are a number of reasons an EPS can be reported differently on websites and publications.

One reason is that some websites and publications

use the "diluted EPS figure." Most UK companies publish an EPS figure and a diluted EPS figure. What the diluted figure actually looks at is any event over the next twelve months that could potentially dilute (create) more shares. For example, Company A above has one hundred million shares in issue. Imagine if its ten directors were each awarded one hundred thousand share options as a bonus. This would mean that at some point during the year, they could exercise their right to get their shares. This would mean there were 101 million shares in circulation, not 100 million, which would, of course, alter the EPS slightly.

A bank that lent the company money may have been given the right to own ten million shares as part of the deal. At any point during the year, the bank could exercise this right, and the company would be forced to create another 10 million shares. This would mean there were 111 million shares in circulation, not the 100 million that we based our EPS out on. That would obviously majorly alter our EPS.

> **Tip:** A rising EPS does not always mean it's automatically a great company. Some companies buy back their own shares rather than growing their business. If the company has less shares in circulation, their EPS is going to rise. EPS is useful to us retail investors, but don't rely on it 100%.

Another reason is that some websites only update the EPS once a year using the annual report, while others use quarterly trading updates to forecast what the current EPS is. This is often referred to as TTM (trailing twelve months). This means the website or publication has looked at the earnings reported in the most recent quarterly updates and worked out the most current EPS it can over the last twelve-month period. This is hard work, especially for re-tail investors like you and me, so I advise you to go with the flow and go with the company's own EPS figures.

At the end of the day, it's not important for us to get fixated with what exact EPS figure we are look-ing at. Obviously, if we have the choice, I would go for diluted EPS and TTM EPS, as they give us more detailed and up-to-date information, but it really doesn't matter that much. What does matter is that you use a single website or source for all your EPS data. It's no good getting one EPS reading from one website that used diluted EPS, and then getting an-other EPS reading for another company not using diluted EPS, and then comparing the two.

Make sure you always compare like with like. As long as your broker or preferred website or publica-tion for financial information keeps their data up to date, using the same calculations across their whole platform (and I'm sure they do), then don't worry about what specific EPS you are using.

So that's EPS. I told you it was easy. It's an amazing, simple little ratio used by professional investors and retail investors alike. A quick glimpse at an EPS ratio can tell you a lot about a company and its size and profitability. However, it does have its limitations, and we obviously need more information to help us on our stock-valuing journey.

The main thing EPS does not look at is the price we have to pay to buy shares. A company may have a terrible EPS, but if it's really cheap (low share price), it may still be attractive as a long-term investment. We need some sort of ratio that tells us whether the price we are paying for those earnings is high or low. Something like a P/E (price to earnings) ratio would be good right now.

**Tip:** Remember, growth is not free. This sounds obvious, but the stock market has a habit of getting very excited and forgetting this basic rule. If a company is growing rapidly, you can expect its costs and overheads to grow rapidly as well. This should be expected and is normal.

For example, it's great if a car manufacturer is going to double in size in the next twelve months, but they will also need double the amount of raw materials, staff, factory space, and so on to facilitate this growth. Always remember, growth is not free, and costs will go up alongside profits!

## P/E ratios (price to earnings)

A P/E ratio (sometimes called the P/E multiple) is by far the most common indicator of value in the stock market. It's used by just about everybody, and it's everywhere you look. But what is it, and why would we want to use it?

The P/E ratio is the quickest and most simple way to find a cheap company. Notice I use the word *cheap* and not *undervalued*. It's a little more complicated than that, but the P/E ratio is a great little tool and should be given a prominent position in every retail investor's toolbox.

The good news is you will never have to calculate your own P/E ratio. It's done for you and is published just about everywhere; however, it's important that you understand what it is and how to calculate it so that you can also begin to understand its strengths and weaknesses.

Calculating a P/E ratio is simple. Take a company's current share price, and divide it by the EPS (you have not forgotten step 2 already, have you?).

$$\frac{\text{Current Share Price (per share)}}{\text{EPS (Earnings or Profits Per Share)}} = PE\ Ratio$$

For example, if the current share price was two pounds each, and current EPS was 0.20, your P/E ratio would be ten times.

By calculating the P/E ratio, we are looking at the share price in terms of earnings. In the example above, you are paying two pounds per share, or ten times one year's earnings, to own that share.

Let me put it another way. If you pay two pounds per share, it will take you ten years (if company earnings don't change) to get your initial investment back. Most investors think ten years is too long to get their investment back. They may be looking for a return quicker than that.

The big question is, what does this actually tell us? What difference does knowing the P/E ratio make? On its own, probably not a lot.

You should never look at a single P/E ratio in isolation. You need to compare your company's P/E ratio against those of its competitors in the same sector.

### Debenhams versus Marks & Spencer

Get your piece of paper out and write down the P/E ratios as well. Your piece of paper should now start looking a little something like this:

| | Current Price | Market Cap | EPS | P/E Ratio |
|---|---|---|---|---|
| Debenhams | 76.73p | £945m | 7.6p | 10.13 |
| Marks & Spen | 409.45p | £6.8bn | 29.50p | 13.82 |

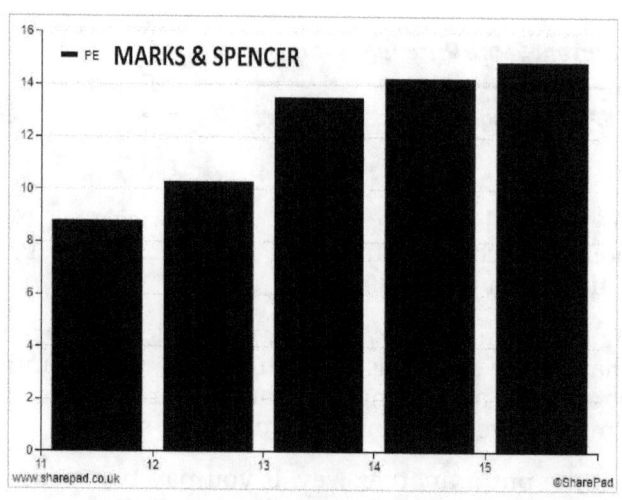

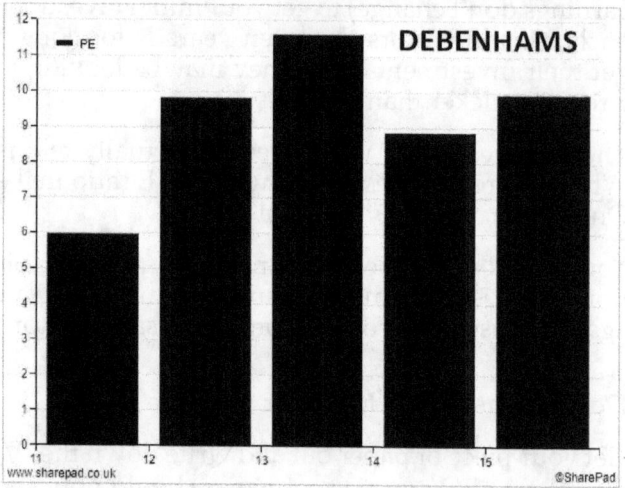

When we look at your comparison table now, we are starting to really understand where each company sits in terms of valuation. Based on the above information, you can see that Debenhams, based on the P/E ratio, is cheaper than Marks & Spencer. If you bought one share in Debenhams, you would only have to wait 10.13 years to get your money back (versus 13.82 years for Marks & Spencer). Although Marks & Spencer has a better EPS than Debenhams, is Debenhams better value for your money in terms of investment? However look at the year-on-year growth of Marks & Spencer. We're starting to build a good picture, and we are asking the right kind of questions, but we need more information.

**Tip:** Remember the stock market is always looking at the future and not just the present or the past. We use the present and the past as a tool to help us understand the company, and help us predict what will possible happen in the future. If a company has performed poorly over the last 5 years, it's unlikely to post amazing results unless a huge amount of work has been done by its current managerial team.

The stock market will always judge a company on its future prospects, not its current trading performance.

If you invest in a company that's got an amazing history, but its future outlook is terrible, your investment will probably lose money. In comparison, don't hold back from investing in a company that you think is undervalued and has amazing prospects, just because its 5 year EPS and PE Ratio is jumping all over the place!

Remember the stock market will always view a stock on future earnings and likely performance over the next 3 to 5 years, not the past 3 to 5 years! We are using past performance to help us understand the current position of the company, and to help us make an informed decision about its likely future performance.

## Loss-making companies and P/E ratio

You will often come across a company that does not have a P/E ratio. That's because the company is loss making and has no earnings. Although it is technically and mathematically possible to work out a negative P/E ratio, they are not accepted by the financial industry and are classed as invalid or irrelevant. That's not to say that you won't see the occasional negative P/E ratio calculation, but more often than not, it will be left blank or have N/A next to it. Don't get too hung up on this. We are retail investors who are trying to grab a quick snapshot of a company, so if it has a negative P/E, just make a note of it, and move on. We will have a brief look at how to value a loss-making company in the conclusion to phase1, so hold tight if this is a particular area of interest for you; we will get there!

## Compare the P/E as much as possible

You don't have to compare the P/E ratios of just two companies. You can compare P/E ratios of several companies or even the average for the whole sector. FT, Bloomberg, or any other decent financial website will give you a P/E sector average. For example, if the general-retailers sector as a whole has a P/E ratio of eighteen times, Marks & Spencer (at fourteen times) may look like a decent value.

Another thing we can look at is the average P/E ratio of every stock in the FTSE 100. For example, if the average FTSE 100 stock trades at a P/E ratio of ten times, and Marks & Spencer is fourteen times, maybe we are looking at the wrong sector if we want the cheapest possible shares. Maybe we'll put Marks & Spencer on our watch list, and if the share price drops for any reason, we may buy it when its P/E ratio reaches eleven or ten times.

But what about the new stores Debenhams are going to open or the new product ranges at Marks & Spencer? This is one of the fundamental weaknesses of P/E ratios. They are good at giving us cold hard facts about what is happening right now, but they don't apply any other logic or give us any other sort of information.

## Very low or very high P/E ratios

If a stock is trading on a very low P/E ratio, don't automatically assume that it's undervalued and you should buy it. Think about why the P/E ratio could be low. Is there a problem with the company? For example, it could be involved in a price war with its competitors, or maybe a new competitor has come along that is gaining rapid market share. We will do all this research in later steps, so don't worry about this at the moment. I'm just trying to stop you from throwing the book down and going on a rampage of buying every share you can find with a low P/E ratio. A stock may be trading on a low P/E ratio because the market is expecting its earnings to fall.

Also, don't discount stocks that have high P/E ratios. If a stock has a high P/E ratio, it could mean the market is expecting earnings to grow dramatically in the near future. For example, many technology stocks that have never made significant profits can trade at seemingly ridiculous P/E ratios. In the United States, stocks like Amazon and Netflix have traded on P/E ratios of several hundred or even one thousand. Investors don't buy Amazon at a P/E ratio of one thousand times because they are happy to wait one thousand years to get their money back. They expect rapid growth in Amazon's earnings.

It may be a good idea to own a share that's about to experience rapid growth in its earnings, or it may be dangerous. During the recent dotcom boom, just about every stock that had anything to do with the Internet started trading on huge P/E ratios. Most of these companies could never justify such huge P/E ratios or even have a business plan to match it, and, of course, we all know how the dotcom boom ended.

**Tip:** Overreliance on P/E ratios will lead you into trouble. They are excellent at giving you one part of the story, but you need the whole story to be a good investor.

Just because a stock used to trade at a P/E of twenty-two times and now trades at fifteen times does not mean it's cheap. There could be a whole host of reasons why it's fallen. Maybe the company has sold part of its business and lost those earnings; maybe it is losing market share to a competitor; or maybe the whole market has topped, and all shares are falling across the board.

P/E ratios are static and don't take into account any qualitative data. Use them, understand them, but do not 100 percent rely on them.

One last thing about P/E ratios. If you want to work them out yourself so you are 100 percent sure you know what's what, that's fine. In fact, that's great. However, if you are like me and don't have that much time on your hands, you may want to use the published P/E ratios on broker websites, in newspapers, or from other sources of information. Again, don't get too concerned if a company's P/E is slightly different on one website than the next. Some websites are slow to update prices, some use live prices to calculate a P/E, and some don't. Again, think back to the EPS and how some analysts use diluted EPS, and some don't; some use TTM EPS, and some don't. All this has a knock-on effect for P/E ratios.

Don't get too hung up on this. Just make sure the website you are using is kept up to date and that you aren't looking at a P/E from the 1980s, and always compare like with like. Don't use a P/E from Debenhams from one website and a P/E for Marks & Spencer from a different one. As long as you compare like with like, you should be OK.

So the trick is to use a P/E ratio as one tool in your investing toolbox. It may be one of the most important tools, like a hammer or a screwdriver, but it's not your only tool. On its own, a P/E ratio can be brilliant and give you an instant understanding of the level of value you are buying a share at, but it can also hide and distort a whole wealth of other information that you need to analyse before making any investment decisions.

## Key points from step 3

- Company earnings (profits) eventually drive everything. You may have to wait, but eventually the stock market will reward good earnings with a higher share price. As long as we bought shares at the right time, this is when we make our money!

- Check the EPS level. Does it look healthy, and how does it compare with its competitors in the same sector?

- Check the historic EPS level. Is the company showing consistent year-on-year growth?

- If you want to, you can compare EPS against the whole sector and the whole market.

- Check the P/E ratio.

- Compare the P/E ratio against competitors in the same sector, the index, and even the market as a whole.

- Always use the same source for your EPS and P/E ratios so you know they have been calculated in the same way.

- Remember the stock market judges a company on its likely future performance. Looking at historical earnings helps us understand the current business, and shows how likely the company performance is to improve or decline in the future.

On that note, we probably need another tool to help us on our investment journey. Let's have a look at price-to-book ratios.

# Step 4:
## Price-to-Book Ratio

You might now be thinking, "We're already getting quite good at this stock-valuing game. We are only on step four, and we know about current share prices and market caps, and we understand the business and sector our chosen investment is in. Our stock has a strong brand and pricing power; it's got a high EPS and low P/E ratio. What can go wrong if we buy it? We just need to find a few more similar stocks, and, "Rodney, this time next year, we'll be millionaires."

I have to agree to a certain extent. We have made a good start, and if you start applying the knowledge you have gained, you will be a better investor. However, we are still a fair distance from being able to make a correct judgement about the value of a company or share price. There are lots more factors to think about.

### What are book value and the price-to-book ratio?

Book value literally indicates the value of a business according to its "books." So if you were to add together all the assets it owns, that gives you a "book value."

Take Marks & Spencer, for example. We have not considered that it's an established business (has the largest market cap, for example), owns shops and car parks, and has land all over the United Kingdom. The company's land and shops and tills and shelves and delivery trucks and so forth all have value. Even if Marks & Spencer went bust and had to sell all its assets on eBay, it would still have a value. If you were thinking about buying the whole business, you would want to get some feel for its actual underlying value.

Let me put it another way. Let's work out the book value of a chap named Sam. Sam is twenty-five years old, his favourite food is curry, and he lives alone in Nottingham (none of that is relevant, but I thought it was interesting). In theory, Sam's life has a book value. He may own 50 percent of his house, and it may be worth £100,000. Sam only owns 50 percent, so £50,000 worth of his house, and has a mortgage for the rest. Sam owns a car worth £10,000. He owns furniture worth £10,000, and he has savings and investments worth £10,000. In this case we can add together the value of Sam's house (not including his mortgage) the values of his car and furniture, and his savings and decide he has a book value of £80,000. To put it another way, buying Sam's life, if judged purely in financial terms, would cost £80,000. At this point we aren't interested in the fact that Sam has a job, which guarantees him income for the next twenty years. We are just looking at a current book value of his life.

To become a good investor and understand if you are buying a stock that is undervalued or overvalued, you need to understand the book value of the business and how much per share you are paying for that book value.

## Calculating price-to-book ratio

So how do we work out a price-to-book ratio? The great news is that you never have to, as it's already done for you and available across a range of websites, newspapers, and other publications. However, I want to spend some time understanding how to calculate a price-to-book ratio and getting to know what's happening behind the scenes. It's only by knowing how it's calculated that you can begin to understand its strengths and weaknesses.

The first thing we need is a book value. For Marks & Spencer, let's start by going around to each and every shop in the country, measuring how many square feet the site is, and then visiting local estate agents and working out the value of one square foot of land in the local area. Then we'll multiply the shop square footage by the number given to you by local estate agents, and then...well, then...OK, you got me. I'm only joking! Now is not the time for a nationwide road trip.

If you started to get angry halfway through that paragraph, you are still awake (good for you). If you did not, you need to start concentrating a little harder!

The easiest way to find a book value is to open the company accounts (don't worry; I will explain all about company accounts and where to find them a little later in step 10) and find the balance-sheet page. In the balance sheet, the company will give you its book value of assets. Yeah, it really is that simple.

Now the suspicious among you will be thinking, "How can we trust the company's own book value?" After all, companies could, in theory, inflate their book values to make their value and stock prices look more attractive. The answer to that is yes, they can. Welcome to the world of investing. There are thousands of ways a company can manipulate its figures and hide all sorts of nasty bits of information. Professional investors get caught by this all the time (look at Enron, for example), so as a retail investor, you stand no chance. Don't even try to fight against this.

You have to remember that it's against the law for companies to manipulate their accounts, and they have to be audited by an independent outside auditor. As a retail investor, you need to assume the companies are giving you the right information, and remember that it's against the law for them to mislead people.

If you don't go with the flow and trust their numbers, you will never invest in anything and will slowly go mad. This is one of the reasons why we won't always get everything right. This is why even after we have done all the research, we still have to use stop-losses and protect against share-price drops. If this were easy, everybody would be doing it, and everybody would be rich.

I also hope you now understand why I insist on showing you how to work out each ratio when you don't need to know how to. By knowing how each ratio is calculated, you will understand its strengths and weaknesses and understand that you need to use all these ratios as a guide, not as gospel.

Anyway, back to our price-to-book ratio. Once you have found the line on the balance sheet that reads "Book Value," take that figure, and write it down.

The next thing you need is the number of shares in issue (remember market caps in step 2). Again, you will easily find this information. It's everywhere, including on the company website and on just about every serious financial website.

Now divide the book value by the number of shares in circulation, and this will give you book value per share.

For example, if a company has a book value of £15 million and has ten million shares in circulation, the book value would be 1.5.

$$\frac{£15,000,000 \text{ book value}}{10,000,000 \text{ shares in circulation}} = 1.5 \text{ book value per share}$$

But this is only half the ratio. We are looking at price-to-book ratio, so we need to factor in the current price. All you do is take the current share price and divide it by the book value per share (the number we just calculated above).

For example, if the current share price was two pounds, the formula would look like this:

$$\frac{£2.00 \text{ current share price}}{1.5 \text{ book value per share}} = 1.333 \text{ price to book ratio}$$

What is this telling us? What does a price-to-book ratio actually mean? Is 1.333 high or low?

Let's stop and think about this for a second. In theory, every book value should be 1.00. If a price-to-book ratio is lower than 1.00, in theory, you are buying shares at a price that is below the company's book value.

Let's go back to the example about Sam at the start of this chapter. In theory, if Sam had a price-to-book ratio below 1.00, we could buy all his assets for less than they are worth. If we paid more than a price-to-book ratio for Sam's assets, then we would be paying more for them than we would get if we separated all his assets and sold them individually.

> **Tip:** There are some stocks and sectors where the price-to-book ratio is crucial, and it is your major tool in understanding their value.
>
> For example, holding companies are the names given to shell companies. Shell companies often don't have any type of business or assets at all. They simply own shares of other companies. In theory, their book value should always trade at exactly 1.00. Nothing more, and nothing less.
>
> Similarly, with listed investment-trust stocks, you should pay a lot of attention to price-to-book ratios.

In theory, every stock in the world should trade at a book value of 1.00, but when you think about all those technology stocks that trade at a P/E of one thousand, they probably have few assets at all (a rented office and a website, for example), so their book value will be terrible. We need to use book value as one of our tools for calculating overall value, but it's not the only factor.

For some asset-rich sectors, like utility companies

and investment-trust companies, the calculation of price-to-book ratios is crucial. But this isn't the case in other sectors like technology, where you are looking for sales growth, earnings, and dividends.

## Debenhams versus Marks & Spencer

So let's get our piece of paper out and add price-to-book ratio as well, and it may start to look something like the following:

|  | Current Price | Market Cap | EPS | P/E Ratio | Price/ Book |
|---|---|---|---|---|---|
| Debenhams | 76.73p | £945m | 7.6p | 10.13 | 1.11 |
| Marks & Spen | 409.45p | £6.8bn | 29.50p | 13.82 | 2.66 |

Now we are building up a fantastic understanding of the value of each share. Marks is trading at 409p, which is the higher share price of the two, and has good earnings (EPS 29.7p) but is trading at over two and a half times price-to-book ratio.

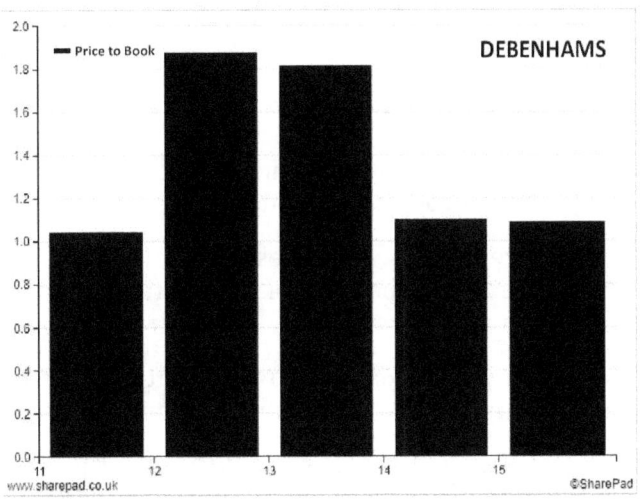

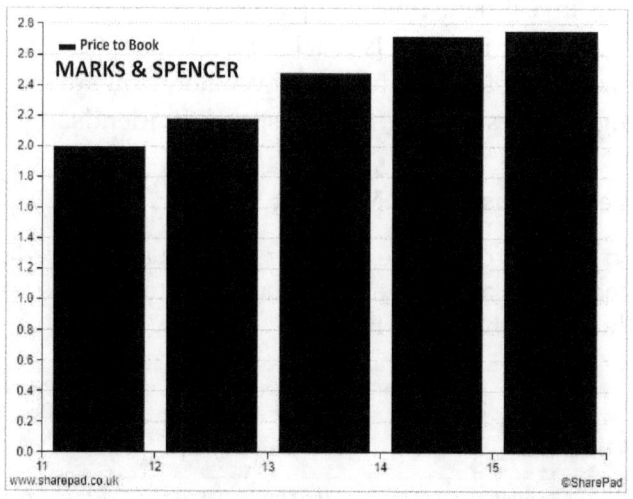

In comparison, Debenhams is trading at a lower P/E ratio and has a price-to-book ratio of just over one. At first, Marks looked like the better bet, as earnings were higher; however, Debenhams is winning in P/E ratio and price-to-book value. Debenhams is beginning to look like the more undervalued stock of the two. We can't make that conclusion yet, though. We need more information.

## Key points from step 4

- Book value literally indicates the value of a business according to its "books."

- Price-to-book compares the book value of a business to the price of buying that business on a per-share basis.

- You will never have to work out book value yourself; it's always done for you.

- In theory, all stocks should trade at a book value of 1.00, and anything less is undervalued, but it's not that simple.

- Price-to-book ratio gives you an instant view as to where the shares are trading against a company's underlying value.

- Price-to-book ratio is not useful on its own, but it is useful when used alongside a number of other ratios and research.

At this point, you still need to keep an open mind. These ratios are great and give an instant picture of how a company is doing. But there are a million other factors to consider, and we haven't even started to look into the future.

For now, let's continue our valuation journey and look at a ratio that sounds terrifying: EV/EBITDA. Anything that sounds that horrible must be impossible to understand, right?

# Step 5:

# EV/EBITDA

What is EV/EBITDA? It's basically another ratio you can use to try to understand if a share is overvalued or undervalued. The easiest way to think about EV/EBITDA is as a P/E ratio on steroids.

**What is enterprise value?**

To work out the value of a company, you need to list every single one of its assets and calculate the price of each one. However that's an amazing amount of work so accountants use a shortcut! EV stands for enterprise value, which accountants would describe as equity (provided by shareholders) plus debt (provided by banks or lenders) minus cash.

However, we are not accountants, so let's put it this way. Companies that are listed on the stock exchange have two main ways of raising money. First of all, they sell shares (or other types of financial instruments) to investors and raise money that way. The second way is to borrow money from banks or other types of lenders. Basically, the enterprise value of a company is the total amount of money it has raised minus its current cash. The theory is, if you know how much the company spent on assets, you also know the value of the assets. Instead of compiling a long list of assets and their value, you just look at how much money has been spent by the business, and deduct any cash and hey presto, you have an enterprise value!

Let me put it another way, and let's talk about Sam (our curry-loving twenty-five-year-old friend from Nottingham) again. Sam plays five-a-side football on Monday nights and likes Coronation Street. Again, that's not particularly relevant, but I thought it was interesting.

We could value Sam's life by going through his individual assets like we did in step 4. Another way of valuing Sam's life is to look at where he gets his money from. After all, he can't just conjure things up out of thin air. He has to pay for them. If we know where the money is coming from and how much is going in, we can calculate Sam's enterprise value. Sam borrowed £100,000 mortgage to buy his house, but he has £10,000 of savings in his bank account. You can calculate his enterprise value as £90,000 (100K - £10K = £90K).

Still struggling? Let me put it another way. You go out for a meal with friends and pay for the whole night. You could work out how much you spent by working out how much each meal cost, how much each dessert cost, how much the drinks were, how much the tip was, how much the taxi was there and back, and so forth. Another way to value the night out would be to think that you got £200 out of the Cashpoint machine before you went out. You now have £50 left, so the night's value was £150.

To go back to the investment world, take all the money a company has raised by selling shares and all the money it has borrowed from lenders, add them together, and then take away its current cash situation. Hey, presto, you have an enterprise value.

To work out an enterprise value of a company, you simply take the market cap (number of shares in issue times current share price) and add the net debt (all company debt) minus cash.

## What's EBITDA?

So that's the EV bit sorted, but what's the other bit about? EBITDA is a profit or earnings figure. The EB stands for "earnings before," so that's easy! The ITDA stands for interest, tax, depreciation, and amortization.

Wow. I promised to write a book without any financial jargon in it, and then I go and pull out a sentence with the words *interest, tax, depreciation, and amortization* in it. Well, it's really not as bad as it sounds.

There are a few ways that companies can trick investors and hide some dodgy stuff, so investors have fought back and asked to look at the profit a company makes before it's messed about with things like depreciation and amortization.

Interest and tax are pretty straightforward. I think we all know what they are (after all, there are only two certain things in life, death and taxes).

But pure accountants argue that a company can't really control interest rates, taxes, and so forth, so we should not include them in a ratio to see if a stock is over- or undervalued. So by taking interest and tax out of the calculation, you get a purer picture of how the company is doing.

## What are depreciation and amortization?

Depreciation and amortization are interesting, even if they sound boring. They're ways companies can put positive or negative spins on their accounts. For example, let's assume Debenhams goes and buys a new delivery truck for £100,000 but expects to get ten years' use out of it.

At this point, life gets interesting, as companies have a choice of how they account for that £100,000 investment. They can put that £100,000 all into this year's annual accounts, or they can argue that the delivery truck will last ten years and put £10,000 in each year. They could even argue that the truck will probably be worth £20,000 in ten years and that they'll be able to sell it for that amount. So, in fact, they value the £100,000 truck at £80,000 and spread the cost over ten years. You can probably see the ways that companies can hide things, or at least dress them up.

Just for the record, amortization is the expression given to accounting for the value of intangible company assets (assets that are owned but that aren't physical assets like buildings, lands, or trucks). For example, a company's brand, research and development, goodwill, patents, trademarks, copyrights, business agreements, and so forth are all intangible assets. The value of these intangible assets may change over time, and this changing value is referred to as amortization.

Just to be 100 percent clear about amortization, let's pretend a company has a patent worth £1 million for ten years. In year one, you could claim the patent is an asset worth £1 million (has ten years left), but in year two you could argue that patent is worth £900,000 as it now only has nine years left and has lost £100,000 in value.

The way I always remember it is that *depreciation* is the phrase associated with accounting for assets you can physically touch and feel—like cars, trucks, buildings, and so forth. These are often referred to as tangible assets (just because we need more big words; they help us feel clever). *Amortization* is the phrase associated with accounting for assets you can't physically touch—like goodwill and brand. These are also often referred to as (you guessed it) intangible assets.

As a retail investor, you need to know what depreciation and amortization are, but you can't really control them or analyse them without an accounting degree, ten helpers, and lots of spare time. So that's why the EV/EBITDA number is such a good friend to you and why I bring it to your attention.

## P/E ratio versus EV/EBITDA ratio

There are many people in the stock-valuation game who can't get comfortable with the idea that company directors can play around with numbers to this extent. In reality, a company's "brand" or "goodwill" is only worth as much as somebody is willing to pay for it, so it's impossible to put a realistic figure on it. For this reason, many analysts hate the idea of valuing a company with all this fluffy guesswork going on, so they prefer to remove it. EV/EBITDA is the P/E ratio with all the dodgy stuff taken out, which some analysts believe makes it a purer figure that is a little more accurate.

Let's do a direct comparison between our old friend, the P/E ratio, and our new friend, EV/EBITDA.

For a P/E ratio, you are comparing the current share price against earnings. But why are you using only the current share price? This is basically the market cap, so you are only using the shares in issue for a company. Why are you only looking at shareholder capital and not at other lenders, like banks or business loans and so on? What if a company has huge debt but has a small market cap? This means you are analysing the business using a small market cap and not even starting to consider the large bank loans. (Don't worry; we'll do a lot on debt in step 7.)

Also, the P/E ratio looks at EPS or company profit (earnings) after tax. But different companies pay different taxes in different ways. Should you really be concerned about interest when company directors have no control over the Bank of England and the setting of current interest rates? Is it safe to look at and analyse a company that has decided its own depreciation and amortization numbers, given that these numbers can be hugely subjective and differ wildly between different companies? Surely it would be better to strip out all this dodgy stuff.

So that's what EV/EBITDA is. As I said, it's basically a P/E ratio on steroids. Take P/E, add a little more to the P bit to make it more representative, and take some dodgy stuff out of the E bit to make it less open to directors' manipulation (or director overoptimism, should I say?).

## Can you trust the EV/EBITDA figure 100 percent?

So can you trust an EV/EBITDA figure 100 percent? The answer, I'm afraid, is no. If a company is really motivated to hide bad news or bad numbers, they can still hide it in about one million other ways. However, this is true for every single ratio, number, and report we will ever look at, so feel free to use the EV/EBITDA number and trust what it's telling you. Just remember to always have your stop-loss in place — but that goes without saying.

I am sometimes asked if there is a difference between the EBITDA and EV/EBITDA. The answer is no; they are the same thing. The only difference is EBITDA is a stand-alone profit figure, while EV/EBITDA is a ratio where the profit figure has been divided by enterprise value.

## Where to find the EV/EBITDA ratio

There is one last bit of bad news I need to tell you about EV/EBITDA. It's not widely available. Just about every other ratio I talk about is found everywhere, but there is no legal requirement for companies to give you their EBITDA (though nearly all do), and most of the bog-standard financial websites don't report the figure. It's not an impossible number to find, but some websites withhold it unless you sign up for a free trial.

Your broker (the company you use to buy and sell shares) should really also be providing you with up-to-date P/E ratios, EPS, EV/EBITDA, and so on. This can be a case of if you don't ask, you don't get! If they don't provide a good research centre and good support for retail investors, move to a broker that does. You are giving your broker money every time you buy and sell a share, so it might be worth paying a little extra if you can find a broker that provides you with up-to-date research and ratios.

If you don't have access to any brokers accounts or sources of financial data, you will usually find the EV/EBITDA number published in the company's annual report or on their website (we will touch on the annual reports in step 10).

As a last resort, if you Google the share you are looking at and then type EV/EBITDA, you will usually find it calculated for you. When you start looking for this ratio, you will find it. Find out if your broker (the company you buy and sell shares with) offers EV/EBITDA ratios, and if they don't, think about switching to one that does.

### Debenhams versus Marks & Spencer

Once you have found the magical number, you need to add it to your sheet of paper, which may look a little something like this:

|  | Current Price | Market Cap | EPS | P/E Ratio | Price/ Book | EV/ EBITDA |
|---|---|---|---|---|---|---|
| Debenhams | 76.73p | £945m | 7.6p | 10.13 | 1.11 | 5.1x |
| Marks & Spencer | 409.45p | £6.8bn | 29.50p | 13.82 | 2.66 | 7.8x |

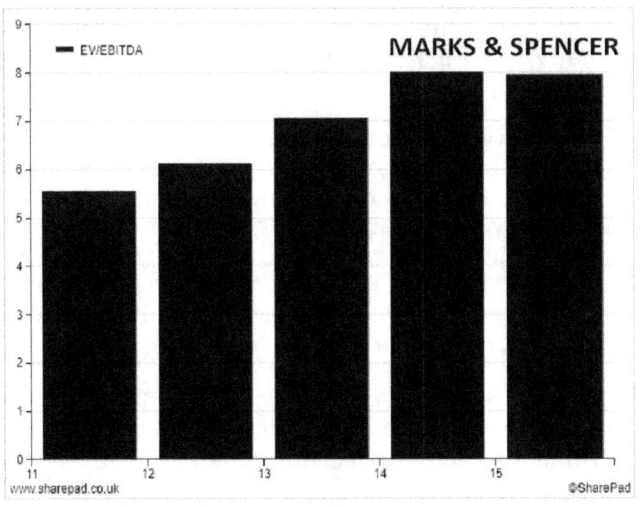

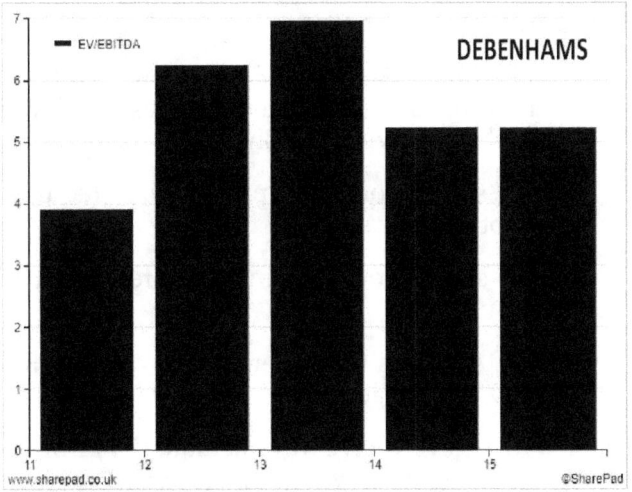

So this is further proof that Marks & Spencer is expensive in comparison to Debenhams. Debenhams has the lowest EV/EBITDA at 5.1 times, so it looks better value in comparison to Marks & Spencer when viewed on this ratio alone.

**Tip:** I am often asked if you should automatically short a stock with a high P/E ratio and EV/EBITDA ratio.

No, absolutely not is always my answer. You need more information. Many stocks trade on high earnings ratios, and the shares go on to justify those ratios and go higher. Xerox in the United States was trading at a P/E of one hundred times in 1959, which looked like great value when the stock rose over 3000 percent in the next few years.

Good investing is a mixture of quantitative and qualitative data. You need to collect all the data and make an overall decision when you can see the whole picture.

### Key points from step 5

- EV/EBITDA is a P/E ratio on steroids. If nothing else, just remember it as a P/E ratio with some wishy-washy stuff stripped out.

- EV stands for "enterprise value" (equity + debt - cash).

- EB stands for "earnings before," so that's easy!

- ITDA stands for "interest, tax, depreciation, and amortization."

- You never have to calculate EV/EBITDA yourself; it's always done for you.

- You can trust an EV/EBITDA figure more than a standard P/E ratio, but never trust it 100 percent.

- EV/EBITDA figures can be hard to find, and you may need to sign up to a website or publication. When finding your next broker, make sure they provide them to you and that they are accurate and up to date.

- Just because a stock has a low P/E ratio or a low EV/EBITDA ratio, that does not mean you should automatically buy it. Also, if a stock has a high P/E ratio or a high EV/ EBITDA ratio, you should not automatically short it. A mixture of quantitative and qualitative data is needed to make good investment decisions.

As I said in the introduction, fundamental analysis and value investing is all about a company's earnings (profits). For this reason, I think we need to switch our thinking away from trying to understand if a company is cheap or not and try to understand how our companies are evolving. Remember what I said earlier in the book, the stock market prices companies on its likely future earnings, not just its past and present earnings.

For the first time, let's try to get an indication about what may happen in the future. After all, we buy shares in the hope that the price will move upwards. All we have done so far is look at where the stock is valued right now, so we are basically looking at the past as a guide to the future. Let's look at earnings growth and the PEG ratio.

# Step 6:
# PEG (Price to Earnings Growth)

We now know how to value a stock given its current performance. We can work out if a share is expensive or cheap in comparison to its competitors, given the information the company supplied in its last company report. However, things can change, companies can get better, and earnings can improve. Obviously, companies can also get worse, and earnings can evaporate. The stock market is always looking at the future and is as concerned about the future as it is about the present. As retail investors, we need some quick-and-easy tools to help us look into the future as well.

## Not all companies can enjoy high growth all the time!

Feel free to skip the next two paragraphs, but I'm going to give a random investor's life lesson. It's important for investors to understand the natural cycle of businesses, sectors, and even countries. It's not unusual for a new business in a new sector to undergo massive growth and trade on massive valuations in its early years. You may feel that paying a P/E of one thousand for a tech company that has never made a profit is stupid, but one hundred years ago, investors were excited and paid the same valuations for the utility companies, railways, then cars, then aeroplanes, and then televisions — all of which were "tomorrow's technology" at some point. Those businesses (and many more) have gone from high growth and exciting businesses and sectors to large, lumbering, low-growth, and boring companies in boring sectors. Companies cannot grow at 25 percent a year forever. If they could, one would have taken over the world by now.

It's exactly the same with countries as well. Look at China, for example. So many people are expecting the Chinese economy to grow at 15 percent a year forever, but it won't, and it can't. Sooner or later, everybody in China will own a house, fridge, freezer, and car, and then where will the growth come from? How will Facebook continue to grow so quickly and aggressively once everybody has a Facebook account? There is a natural flow to these things that is obvious and there for everybody to see, but a huge number of investors refuse to accept this basic and proven concept. They think that their investment or their company is somehow the exception to the rule and will grow at 25 percent a year forever and ever.

If you did skip the last paragraph, you can start here, as the life lesson is over. Looking into the future and trying to forecast how a company will perform is essential for any investor, and, let's be honest, this separates the adults from the children.

## What is PEG; do I need a clothesline?

The PEG ratio is the stock market's most well-known, well-used, and basic ratio for looking into the future. It is basically an extension of the P/E ratio and adds earnings growth onto it.

The PEG ratio is brilliant if you are one of those investors who believe in a direct link between company earnings and share price. I could go one step further. There are those in the market who believe that the current price of a share is all the company's future earnings squeezed together in one efficient calculation.

To put it a different way, you could argue that a house is only worth the total rental income you can squeeze from it during its lifespan. So if you could only squeeze £100,000 from the future rental value of your home, you should not pay more than £100,000 for it. That's a little extreme, but you have to understand this idea if you want to know how to interpret PEG.

Let's look at the ratio, and all this theory will start to make sense. To calculate a PEG, you need the current P/E ratio of the company. Let's say that Company X trades on a P/E ratio of ten times.

You now need the company's earnings growth rate in percentage terms. If Company X's EPS is 0.10 per share this year, but the company is forecast 0.11p a share next year, you can see that the growth rate is 10 percent.

Now divide the P/E ratio by the percentage earnings growth, and you get your PEG.

$$\frac{PE\ ratio = 10x}{EPS\ growth = 10\%} = PEG\ ratio = 1.00x$$

Or, to put it in English, ten divided by ten is one.

What does this actually tell us? On its own, this is an absolutely brilliant piece of information! If the PEG is one, that means that, in theory, the company's valuation is fair. The share price and PEG are in perfect harmony, and you are paying the right price for a share.

If the PEG is less than one, then the company looks cheap. Basically, this means that the company is trading below the price of its future earnings, and you should buy it.

If the company is trading above a PEG of one, in

theory, it's expensive, as it's trading at a price that is higher than its future earnings.

## So the PEG ratio can be interpreted like this:

PEG 0.5 or less = Strong buy (We are going to get rich on this one!)

PEG 0.5 to 1 = Buy (It's undervalued, and shares will go up when the market realizes its mistake.)

PEG 1 = Neutral (This is the correct value of the shares.)

PEG 1 to 2 = Sell (It's overvalued; get rid of it.)

PEG 2 or above = Strong sell (Go short, and send the kids to private school; we have a future winning lottery ticket.)

So let's put some meat on the bones and give you an example.

Company A has a P/E Ratio of 20, and a growth rate of 15%, the company would have a PEG Ratio of 1.33 (20/15 = 1.33)

Company B has a P/E Ratio of 40 and a growth rate of 50%, the company would have a PEG Ratio of 0.80 (50/40 = 0.80)

So as you can see from the above example, if you were just looking at earnings and the P/E Ratio, you would buy Company A because its P/E Ratio is significantly lower than Company B. However when also looking at future earnings, you will see Company B represents better value because its trading below one.

Oh, but only if it were this easy. Trust me; it's not. The big problem some of you will notice is that bit I slipped in about future earnings growth. In the first example above (inside the grey box), I said EPS would go from 0.10 to 0.11, but where did I get that from, and can we be sure that's actually going to happen?

The earnings growth is a forecast made by city analysts. These are the incredibly clever people who earn the big bonuses at investment banks. They get paid for bringing together all their knowledge about the company, the sector that company is in, the current and future economic climate, and a whole host of other factors including (and by no means exclusive to) potential government legislation and new competitors joining the sector.

Stock analysts try to piece together this jigsaw of information and do the best they can to predict the future performance of each and every company they analyse. Add to the cooking pot a dash of mergers and acquisitions and trying to factor in the motivations and personalities of an individual company's management, and you really have the perfect definition of an impossible task. (This is why the good ones are worth their weight in gold and earn the big bonuses.)

City analysts get these predictions wrong. In fact, they get them wrong a lot. The bad ones get them wrong most of the time, and the good ones get them wrong some of the time. But let's be honest; city analysts know more about these stocks than we do. City analysts may get future EPS rates horribly wrong, and they may not foresee the company managing director falling ill and taking early retirement, but they are in a better place to give it a go than we are. These analysts go to all the company meetings, they meet and chat with the company's managers, they talk to large institutional investors, and they have access to realms of information we retail investors don't.

### PEG is the friend of the retail investor!

As a retail investor, a PEG ratio is an essential tool. Even if I can't convince you to trust and love this tool, it gives you a crucial insight as to what the professionals are thinking and why the share prices are trading in the way they are.

### Why can I find different PEGs if I look in different places?

PEGS are available all over the web, but again, they can wildly differ from one website to the next. This is for a number of reasons, the first being that it's a little unambitious to look only one year ahead like we did in the example above, so some PEGs are calculated using two, three, four, or maybe five years of earnings–growth predictions. Predicting earnings five years ahead is significantly harder than pre-

RICHARD MORGAN

dicting earnings two years ahead, so some analysts release different timescales on PEGs. This is an important point, because some sectors favour long-dates PEGs, like in established sectors where there is a consistent history and the sector is not changing rapidly. I would rather try to predict the long-term earnings growth of a dull, boring, established electricity or water utility company than try to predict what smartphone sales will be like in 2020. However, ironically, PEGs are not that useful for old, established, low-growth companies, as these often pay decent dividends, which are not factored into PEG at all (just wait for step 8).

Another reason a PEG may be different on one website or publication than another is that they use different growth forecasts. An investment bank, for example, will calculate and use its own growth-rate forecasts. A general market-information provider may use an average of all the forecasts. So you can see that there are a number of different ways to calculate a PEG.

As a retail investor, don't get caught up by this. Just understand how the PEG you are looking at is calculated, and make sure you always compare like for like (use the same website or financial publication if you are comparing one company's PEG with another company's). Again, this is what your broker is for. Speak to your broker and understand how they calculate their PEG rates. If your broker does not provide PEG rates, find a broker who does!

**PEG relies on analysts' forecasts; they can get their forecasts wrong**

I want to red-flag something at this point. I always tell retail investors, "Don't trust anybody," and this is an excellent example. Some investment banks earn a considerable amount of money by advising companies. They may provide lending to that business, or they may manage the process of an IPO (initial public offering), takeover, stock split, or a million different other things. This is a sensitive relationship between the investment bank and the company, and competition for each client is fierce. Investment banks often compete with each other to win this type of business.

It would be a little awkward if an investment bank that was advising a company to issue new shares to investors were then to publish a research document saying, "Sell," and claiming terrible times were ahead with no growth forecast. Investment banks will strenuously argue that there would be no pressure put on their analysts to make companies' positions look more rosy, and they would shout about the fact that there are walls in place so that the two different areas of the investment bank are not allowed to talk to each other, but I will let you make up your own mind.

Don't make your mind up yet; we discuss this again in step 13.

If you can only find one PEG for a business, make sure it wasn't calculated by an investment bank that is also an adviser to the business. It may (or may not) create an overly positive picture. Again, I will show you how to investigate who is advising companies and what to look out for in steps 10 and 13.

## Debenhams versus Marks & Spencer

So let's get our piece of paper our again, and now let's look at what difference PEG ratios make to the overall picture. It could now look like this:

| | Current Price | Market Cap | EPS | P/E Ratio | Price/Book | EV/EBITDA | PEG (5-year) |
|---|---|---|---|---|---|---|---|
| Debenhams | 76.73p | £945m | 7.6p | 10.13 | 1.11 | 5.1x | 3.08 |
| Marks & Spen | 409.45p | £6.8bn | 29.50p | 14.82 | 2.66 | 7.8x | 1.71 |

Now that puts the cat among the pigeons. We can understand why Debenhams is trading at a much lower P/E, price-to-book, and EV/EBITDA than Marks & Spencer. It's one thing to buy a share because it's cheap; it's quite another to buy a cheap share with poor earnings growth. We can now understand that the future for Debenhams may not be that bright, and that's why its value is lower. If at the end of phase 1 we are still interested, we can conduct further research to try to build the story around Debenhams and understand why earnings–growth forecasts lead to a PEG of 3.08. Marks is hardly cheap at a PEG of 1.71. It seems the current share price of 409 pence per share is not taking into account that analysts are expecting earnings to fall over the next few years.

PEG is not perfect by any stretch of the imagination, but it's a nice little ratio to try to understand the future growth prospects of a company. As retail investors, we should try to get a hold of it and use it.

**Key points from step 6**

- PEG is price to earnings growth; it basically

looks at the share price in relation to predicted earnings growth in the future.

- PEG relies on analysts' forecasts for earnings growth. Analysts can get these wrong, and unforeseen things can happen in the future that affect earnings.

- In theory, every company should trade at a PEG of 1 (parity); below is undervalued, and above is overvalued. But it's not that simple.

- As retail investors, we are looking for shortcuts where possible. PEG gives us the professional investors' opinion about earnings growth, so it's well worth adding to our toolbox!

There is a huge elephant in the room though, something we have not even begun to discuss. What about debt and how much debt a company is in? Should we even look at a company if it has a large amount of debt? Let's move on to step 7 and think about debt.

# Step 7:

# Company Debt, Gearing, and Leverage

Let's cut straight to the chase. I will never buy a company with a poor debt situation, and neither should you! From the work you have done so far, you might find a fantastic company with good earnings and low valuation and a low PEG, but if it's riddled with debt, major red warning lights should go off in your head. It's really difficult to generalize like this, but big debt (that far outweighs its revenues) is dangerous unless the company has a major game changer in the pipeline. That can lead to a whole new set of issues, so leave it alone. There are plenty more fish in the sea.

> **Tip:** Always remember, a company with zero debt will never go bust!

## How much debt is too much debt?

That said, I am not generally put off by large amounts of debt. It's just if the debt is likely to hinder the business or ultimately make it go bust. I think some debt is OK. I just worry when a company has significantly more debt than assets.

Just to play devil's advocate for a second, there are professional investors who would not buy a company with zero debt because they feel the company's management is not trying to expand and grow, so what does that say about long-term growth of the business?

Some investors prefer bank debt over issuing new shares, because, ultimately, it is cheaper (better value) to pay back a bank loan than it is to pay dividends for the rest of the company's life. Also, dividends are paid from posttax profits, but bank interest is paid from pretax profits, so there is a good argument that borrowing money from banks is more beneficial than issuing new shares. Having said all this, most companies in the United Kingdom use a mixture of money from shareholders and money from banks.

So what exactly am I trying to say? Let's assume a company has £1 billion of debt. That sounds like a lot of debt. But it's all relative. If the company has a $20 billion turnover and makes £2 billion profit each year, then a £1 billion level of debt is really no problem at all. It's neither here nor there. However, if a company has a £500 million turnover, £1 billion of debt, and has never made a profit, I walk away. I may be missing the next Amazon or Facebook by not investing, but that's OK with me. I would rather miss out on the one winner (that's like finding a needle in a haystack) than invest in a string of highly indebted, loss-making companies that are always promising a brighter tomorrow but never delivering.

The best thing about analysing a company's debt is that the information is common and available everywhere. OK, I have to bury my head in shame and admit it's not easy finding EV/EBITDA and PEG ratios online unless you sign up for some whizzy website or your broker's website is kept up to date, but the debt ratios I suggest we look at are as common as P/E ratios and are found just about everywhere.

### Net asset value per share

The first thing I want to look at is net asset value (NAV) per share. Don't get stressed and start shouting, "You promised not to use any financial jargon." Net asset value is simply a different way of looking at what a company is worth on the whole. The way to calculate it is a little like the way we calculated book value in step 4. You list the total assets of a company minus all its liabilities.

If a company has assets of £150 million and liabilities (debts) of £100 million, the NAV would be £50 million. On its own, NAV is not really that useful, as we have no idea if £50 million is good or bad and if this helps us understand if a company is overvalued or undervalued. The exception to this rule is a negative NAV. If it is negative, we know straight away that the company owes more than the total of all its assets, and that's a real worry. However, assuming the NAV is not negative, we need to compare its NAV per share.

The way to calculate NAV per share is simple, and you can probably do it yourself by now.

$$\frac{\textit{Net asset value}}{\textit{Total shares outstanding}} = \textit{Net asset value per share}$$

Let's pretend that Company X has a net asset value of £50 million and has one hundred million shares outstanding.

$$\frac{\textit{£50,000,000 net asset value}}{\textit{100,000,000 shares outstanding}} = \textit{0.5p net asset value per share}$$

Again, on its own, the NAV per share figure is not that helpful, but it does give a vague snapshot of how deeply in debt a company is. It's worth noting that some sectors carry more debt than others, and some sectors have lower NAVs than others. The NAV calculation becomes really useful when you start comparing the NAV of one company with its rivals in its own sector. This helps you determine whether your stock has a significant level of debt or not.

It's also worth mentioning that NAV calculations are critical to look at for the valuation of shares in sectors where the value of a company comes from the assets it holds rather than the profit stream generated by the business. The most obvious examples of these are investment trusts and property companies rather than the latest tech businesses that don't really need any assets, just a whizzy website. The NAV is important for stocks like supermarkets (all that land and all those buildings they own), but I would be as interested in earnings.

## Debt ratio

The second tool in your toolbox should be the debt ratio. This is another really simple, quick, and easy ratio that allows you to see at a glance how much debt a company has.

Simply take the long-term and short-term debt and add them together to give you a total debt. Divide this number by the total assets of the company, and multiply by one hundred to make it a percentage.

$$\frac{\text{Short term debt + long term debt}}{\text{Total assets of company}} = \text{Debt raio}$$

For example, Company X has short-term debt of £20 million and long-term debt of £100 million. It also has total assets of £200 million.

$$\frac{\text{£120 million total debt}}{\text{£200 million total assets}} = 60\% \text{ debt ratio}$$

As you can see, the debt ratio can give you a snapshot of exactly how much debt a company has in percentage terms. So 0 percent means the company has no debt, and 100 percent means the company has the same amount of debt as it has assets. In theory, if it was forced to shut down, it would need to sell all its assets to pay back its debt. Above 100 percent means the company has more debt than assets, and this should set off alarm bells during your research. That's not to say you won't buy it, but you need to do your research to make sure there's something in the pipeline that will make significant amounts of money and that the debt is safe and not about to be recalled.

The debt ratio is significant for companies that have a lot of assets, again, like mining companies, supermarkets, investment trusts, and so forth.

Ironically, as I am writing this paragraph, I have just (in the last five minutes) bought shares in a company with a debt ratio of 358 percent. On the face of it, that's a ridiculous decision, but I have done my homework, and I believe in the long-term story. I also have comfort that a large chunk of the debt is owned by a pension fund that also owns 40 percent of the company, so they "probably" won't recall their debt and force the business into liquidation, as it will harm their own shares and investment. The company has been in a mess, and new management has turned it around. I think I will probably hold these shares for the next five to ten years, but it could also go bust next week.

The key thing is that I am going into the investment with my eyes open and aware of the potential problem. I am taking a risk and will watch the debt situation like a hawk, and if it continues to get worse and not better, I will cut and run as fast as I can.

## Leverage

I'm going to throw a new word about, and that is *leverage*. This is the concept of borrowing more money to help you grow faster and make higher returns.

Let me give you an example: Sam, our football-, Coronation Street-, and curry-loving chap from Sheffield who likes going home to his mom and dad every Sunday for a cooked dinner and who sometimes takes his shirts home for his mom to iron. (Again, this isn't relevant, but I thought it was interesting.)

Sam can afford to borrow £200,000 to buy a house for £200,000. However, if he uses leverage, he can borrow more and can maybe afford to borrow £300,000 for a £300,000 house. In the short term, Sam is making his life difficult. The larger mortgage payments will make his life miserable and cut his disposable income right down. But in the long term, his life will be easier by being more leveraged. Once the mortgage is paid off twenty-five years later, he will have a far bigger and more valuable home. If house prices have risen for the last twenty-five years, he will have made a far larger capital gain. So for Sam, as long as he can continue to make his mortgage payments and doesn't lose his job, being highly leveraged will pay off.

> **Tip:** As a retail investor, you can use leverage to buy and sell shares. A number of brokers and trading accounts will let you buy and sell shares using leverage. You can spread bet or trade CFDs (contracts for difference) on leverage. Never trade on leverage unless you 100 percent understand what you are doing!
>
> Spread betting is a modern way to invest. You don't actually buy or sell the shares; you "place a bet" on a share you think is going up

or down, and you only pay or receive the actual amount of money you make or lose. Spread betting has a bad reputation among retail investors, and it's often considered complicated and difficult. Well, it's not easy, but when you understand it, it's a legitimate tool. It allows you to short stocks as well as buy them, and you don't pay tax on capital gains.

Often spread-betting companies have training accounts where you are not actually trading. Others have safety nets so you can't lose more than you put in, and some offer tiny investment sizes (a few pence a move), meaning you can only lose the price of a pint of beer.

However, I repeat, only use leverage if you 100 percent understand what you are doing.

## Debt-to-equity ratio

The debt-to-equity ratio basically looks at how financially leveraged a company is.

Working out the debt-to-equity ratio is simple. Take the company's liabilities (things like bank loans, mortgages, etc.) and divide by the shareholder equity (assets less liabilities), so subtract the company debt from things like cash, stocks, buildings, trucks, and so forth.

$$\frac{\textit{Company liabilities (debts)}}{\textit{Shareholder equity (assets - debts)}} = \textit{Debt-to-equity ratio}$$

For example, Company X has assets of £150 million but debts of £100 million.

$$\frac{\textit{£100 million company liabilities}}{\substack{\textit{£150 million shareholder equity} \\ \textit{(company assets - liabilities)}}} = \textit{0.667 debt-to-equity ratio}$$

A high debt-to-equity ratio is not a good sign. Anything over one is a concern, as it's telling us that the company has more debts then shareholder equity. Like with Sam, this may or may not work out in the long term, so we need to keep our eyes open and have a good think about the company's debt situation and high gearing before we invest.

## Assets-to-equity ratio and cash-to-equity ratio

I have to be honest. I have been debating putting these two ratios in as I don't want to go overboard, but I have decided to mention them because they are both widely available and publicised on websites alongside share prices. If you are going out of your mind with boredom at the moment, feel free to skip this section, as NAV per share, debt ratio, and debt-to-equity ratio, along with the gearing stuff below, is probably enough.

If you are still reading, that means you are keen, so let's look at these two ratios.

Assets-to-equity ratio is calculated by dividing the total assets of the company by shareholder equity. For example, Company X has assets of £250,000 and debt of £100,000. Take the £100,000 of debt away from the £250,000 in assets, and you get £150,000. Divide that by the total amount of assets (£250,000), and you get a ratio of 0.60.

$$\frac{(Assets = £250k - Debt = £100k)}{(Assets = £250k)} = 0.60 \text{ asset-to-equity ratio}$$

To put it in percentage terms, that is 60 percent. This tells us the company owns 60 percent of its assets, and 40 percent are owned by its creditors.

Cash-to-equity ratio is the ratio of a company's cash on hand against its total net worth. It's calculated by dividing the total cash assets of the company by shareholder equity. For example, Company X has £100,000 of cash available after paying all its operational expenditures (the money the business needs to spend to be able to do what it does — things like wages, products, debts, etc.). It also has assets of £250,000. Divide £100,000 by £250,000 to get the cash-to-equity ratio.

$$\frac{(Cash = £100k)}{(Assets = £250k)} \quad 0.40 \text{ cash-to-assets ratio}$$

Again, the higher the better. If you come across a company with a low cash-to-equity rating, you may need to worry about cash flow, particularly if it has a lot of short-term debts. Remember the saying, turnover is vanity, profits are sanity and cash flow is reality. If a company has no cash it can be a major red flag suggesting the company could encounter cash flow problems. A business sometimes cannot convert its profits into cash and this is something we will be looking at in more detail soon!

### Gross and net gearing

For this one, you need to stay alert. If you're dozing

off at the moment or have just been daydreaming about what it must be like to be a daffodil, you need to start concentrating again. I suggest slapping yourself across the face and taking another sip of coffee.

There are two types of gearing: operational gearing and financial gearing. We are interested in financial gearing.

Just for the record, operational gearing is the tool that looks at how sensitive a company is to small changes in profits or costs. Put another way, operational gearing looks at the relationship between fixed costs (costs that don't change, like staff wages, buildings, etc.) and variable costs (costs that do change, like utility bills and resources).

Company X, for example makes £100 million in sales each year. It has fixed costs of £80 million and variable costs of £10 million. In total, it makes £10 million in profit each year. The following year, Company X has a good year and increases sales by 10 percent to £110 million. Fixed costs stay the same at £80 million because they are fixed, and variable costs increase by 10 percent in line with the 10 percent rise in sales. Now Company X has made a profit of £19 million (£110m - £80m - £11m), which means profit has increased by 90 percent when sales only increased by 10 percent. If a business has high operational gearing, small moves can have a dramatic effect on profit. Investment banks have high operational gearing. That's why they make so many staff redundant when times are hard and why they go on huge hiring sprees when times are good. When times are bad, the only thing an investment bank can do is reduce fixed costs and make staff redundant, but when times are good, they are looking for as much boost in sales as possible because it will have a huge effect on profit, so they go hiring.

We are not interested in operational gearing at this

time. We are looking at financial gearing. Financial gearing is essentially used to describe the amount of debt a company has. A company with a lot of debt is often referred to as highly geared.

Working out the gross financial gearing of a business is easy. Simply take all the debt the company has (long-term debt plus short-term debt plus bank overdrafts) and divide it by shareholder equity.

The calculation to work out gross financial gearing would look like this:

**Total Debt**
(long-term debt + short-term debt + bank overdrafts)
──────────────────────────────── = *Gross gearing*
**Total shareholder equity**

Net financial gearing is exactly the same as gross financial gearing, but you take the net-debt figure instead of the gross-debt figure (so you subtract the cash the company has in its bank accounts from its total debts) and divide it by new shareholder equity (company assets minus liabilities).

The calculation to work out net financial gearing would look like this:

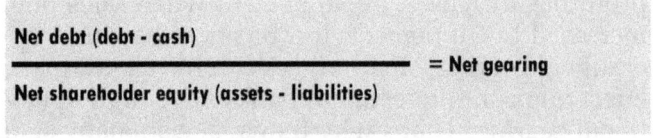

Net debt (debt - cash)
──────────────────────────────── = Net gearing
Net shareholder equity (assets - liabilities)

The financial gross- and net-gearing ratios will always be expressed as percentages, and, as always, you have to keep an open mind and compare your company's stock to the others in its sector to get a true reflection if its gearing is too high or too low. As a general rule, any stock I look at with a gearing below 40 percent is absolutely fine in my opinion. Anything from 40 to 70 percent is a little more serious, and I would need to get my head around it and take a closer look. Anything above 70 percent is a real concern, and I would definitely have a good look at the balance sheet and see the breakdown of long-term debt versus short-term debt to try to understand whom the company owed money to. Being really highly financially geared with loads of short-term debt provided by banks is a real worry and may keep you awake at night.

## Watch out for hidden debt

Finding hidden debt for retail investors is really tricky, but not impossible. What we are looking for is called "off balance sheet debt". This basically means the company owes money which is not being accounted for in their accounts or any of our above ratios.

The most important hidden debt to look out for (in my opinion) is pension fund deficits. If a company owes a huge sum of pension money to its workers, that can be a red flag for investment as far as I am concerned. As a retail investor the techniques needed to identify pension deficits are too advanced for us, this is why my company background check in phase two is so important. If you are seriously going to invest in a company, spend as long as you can searching Google and You Tube for your company's name linked with "Pension Fund Deficit" and see if anything comes up. If you can't find anything, you are probably OK, but if you find pages and pages of news stories about angry trade union leaders demanding more money is put into the pension pot then the company may have a problem.

Another thing you need to try and understand is if the company owns its own assets and properties or does it lease or rent its equipment?

For example a retailer that has hundreds of rented

shops on long term contracts actually has a huge commitment to paying those rents for years ahead (think Woolworths for example). If it gets into trouble and has to close stores, they may have to continue to pay rent meaning the debt will present itself at that point. Does the airline company you want to invest in own its planes, or does it lease them again on a long-term commitment?

Also look out for sale and leasebacks in your chosen investment. If a company is selling its assets and plans to lease them back, it can be an indication that all is not well. Not only that, but sale and leasebacks distort the company's performance as they look cash rich and their profits are higher for a limited amount of time.

A prime example of this was Tesco, who have recently sold stores that they owned outright and have leased them back on long term rental agreements. Tesco went from paying zero rent and being asset rich, to having some long-term rental payments and hidden debts. In return for this transaction Tesco received one off cash payments which made it look like sales and growth were still going OK. On the outside, all looked rosy but on the inside a good company was transforming into a bad one before our very eyes. Any retail investor who googled "Tesco sales and leaseback" would have easily found out this was going on, and stayed away from the investment!

## Marks & Spencer versus Debenhams

I have taken three of the discussed ratios to continue our comparison between our two general retailers.

|  | Debt Ratio | Debt to Equity | Net Gearing |
|---|---|---|---|
| Debenhams | 41.03 | 0.46 | 58.65 |
| Marks & Spencer | 47.43 | 0.58 | 58.46 |

I really don't think there is anything to worry about with the debt situation of either of these two companies. Both are well-balanced, and both have OK debt ratios and debt-to-equity ratios. Indeed when looking at the charts below which is debt expressed as a percentage of market cap, Marks' debt is falling every year which on the outside looks positive. Given the ratios and graphs, there is nothing to worry about regarding balance sheet debt of either company.

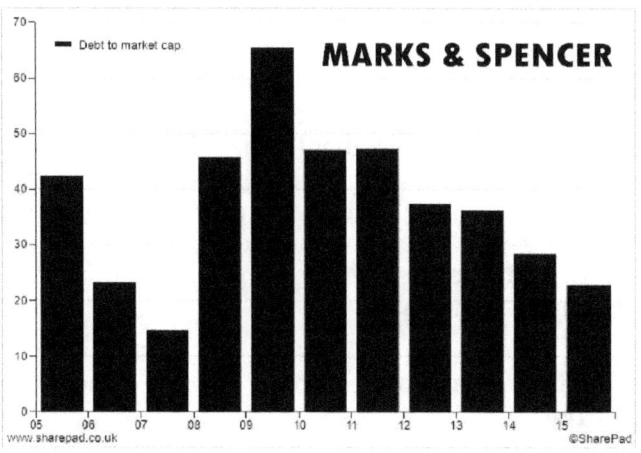

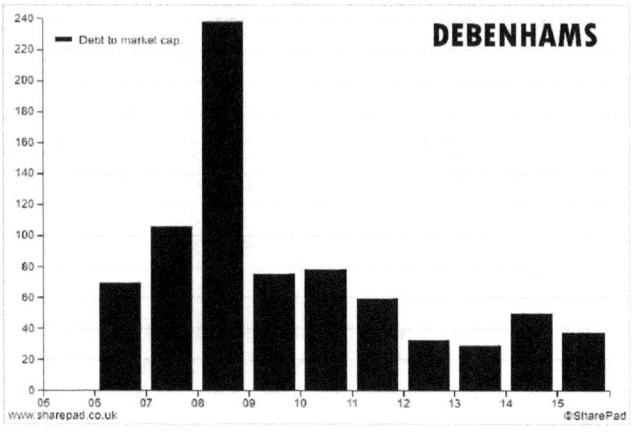

However, spend some time on Google searching for Marks & Spencer and Debenhams and phrases like "sale and leaseback" and "Pension Fund Deficit" and you will see a lot of noise surrounding the companies. In no time at all you will find out that both Debenhams and Marks & Spencer have pension funds totalling over 50% of their market cap. In fact, it looks like all UK retailers have huge pension liabilities so it's a sector wide problem. Debenhams has already conducted a sizeable sale and leaseback and it seems Marks & Spencer are investigating the possibility aswell.

I don't know about you, but I just can't find a compelling reason to buy either Debenhams or Marks & Spencer at the moment. They look reasonably valued with manageable debt but their PEG ratios suggest concern about their future earnings and there is a risk of uncovering some hidden debt at some point. Let's see if we can find anything that can change our mind?

## Final thoughts about company debt, leverage, and gearing

I have given you loads to go on here, and in truth, there are about thirty more useful ratios. However, the ones I have selected give you a fantastic overview of a company and allow you to see, at a glance, whether a company has disproportionate debt or not. All these ratios are common and can be found all over the web and in various publications. Once you know and understand them, you can make informed decisions about companies and their debt levels in seconds.

There is no hard-and-fast rule about debt. Not everybody thinks debt is a bad thing. I am not bothered about investing in a company with serious debt as long as I feel the company can manage it.

If a small company has a financial net-gearing ratio of 200 percent, but its current market cap is small, and I think they have a blockbuster product and will hoover up huge market share and grow rapidly, I may still take a punt and invest. However, this is the exception rather than the rule. The majority of hugely indebted companies will either go bust or will continue to struggle, and you should avoid them like the plague. To put it into context, I buy shares in a company with serious debt only once every two or three years. I will try anything twice, but buying a company with serious debt is the fast path to financial ruin.

If you come across a company with huge debt and you still want to buy it, you really need to be careful. Remove all emotion and be as objective as possible. Think about the worst-case scenario, not the best. Every other part of the business needs to be an absolute blockbuster, and you must not have any other doubts at all about the products, marketplace, company management, competitors, or general condition of the economy and sector. Most importantly, if you invest in a company with high debt, the minute you smell trouble, you must cut and run. Your best friend when it comes to company debt is a decent stop-loss. If you buy a company with loads of debt, and it continues to perform badly, you will eventually lose your money, so get out while you still have some left.

## Key points from step 7

- A company with no debt will never go bust.

- Some company debt is fine; it's when debt is disproportionate to the size of the company that it's a problem.

- Choose two or three of the debt ratios above

to see how much debt the company has.

- Compare the debt level against those of its direct competitors.

- Watch out for hidden debt like pension fund deficits and long-lease property or equipment portfolios.

We are drawing to an end of phase 1 and drawing to an end of building a picture of whether a share is undervalued or overvalued, given its current performance. We will soon be getting into the fun stuff and looking at the "story" of the company and trying to gaze into the future, but for now, we have a couple of sets of numbers we need to look at. First of all we need to look at dividends, and that's what step 8 is all about.

**Step 8:**

**Dividends**

So this is the second-to-last step in phase 1. We are nearly at the end of the boring ratios and mathematics, but we have two final things to think about. The first is dividends, and the promise that companies could send you money every six months as a thank you for buying their shares is really quite enticing.

This is a crucial area, and you really need to understand what a dividend is, how and when it gets paid, and what difference dividends can make to your returns. A stock that pays healthy dividends should make you stop, take notice, and take a closer look. It's worth realizing that stocks that pay dividends nearly always outperform those that don't (as long as the stocks are in the same sector) over the long term. If you are ever faced with two possible buys, and one pays a dividend and one does not, you need some tools to help you understand both companies' valuations.

**Think about the reasons to buy shares in the first place**

So let's go back a few steps and think about the basics of investing in shares. Remember that when you buy a share, you are buying a percentage of a real business, and you will own a part of that business. Always remember that the business is real, employs real people who have real families, and it may be producing real products or services. With this in mind, there tend to be three main reasons to invest in shares.

**Reason 1:** capital gain. You are looking for a return

on your investment. When you buy a house, you hope its value will go up as well as giving you somewhere to live. When buying shares, you hope to buy a share at a low price and sell it at a high price and make a capital gain.

**Reason 2:** income. This is how the company (that you part own, remember) rewards its shareholders by paying dividends. Companies can pay one, two, or even three dividends a year, and, if you hold a big enough stake, dividend payments can offer you a tidy income. There are investors who live off the income dividends pay them.

**Reason 3:** benefits. Another reason some people buy shares is for benefits. For example, some utility companies give their shareholders discounted utility bills, and Eurotunnel shareholders used to get discounted tickets for crossing the channel. I agree that most retail investors would be more interested in reasons 1 or 2, or, in a perfect world, a combination of 1 and 2.

## What can companies do with their profits?

If the company you are interested in buying pays a regular dividend, it's basically giving some of its annual profits directly back to its shareholders (or, in effect, its owners).

It's also worth thinking about the other ways a company could spend the profit it makes.

A.  It could buy back shares, which would lower its market cap. Having a smaller market cap is good for shareholders because if the company continues to make the same profits, all the ratios we have looked at, like EPS and P/E, would be stronger as there are fewer shares to divide the profits between. This would result in the stock becoming under-valued, which would likely lead to a rise in the share price, which would give its share-holders capital gains.

B. It could spend the money by expanding. For example, it could buy a competitor or di-versify away from its core business. This is more difficult to comprehend, as many M&A (merger and acquisition) deals or diversifi-cations (or diworsifications, as Peter Lynch calls them) don't add value to shareholders at all and, in fact, weaken the business.

## Who decides how big dividends are?

Just to be 100 percent clear, it's the directors of the company who decide if the company can pay a div-idend and, if so, how much that dividend will be. You have the right as a shareholder to turn up at the company's annual general meeting (AGM) and argue for a higher or lower dividend payment, but unless you own around 25 percent of the company, you probably won't be listened to. However, some AGMs do have great free tea and coffee, and some even provide biscuits, so it's always worth attend-ing if you have nothing better to do.

It also worth knowing that there are a significant number of investors who strongly agree that busi-nesses should pay profits directly back to sharehold-ers in the form of dividends, rather than spend them on buybacks or expansion plans. Many successful investors and professional fund managers invest only in dividends and dividend returns, so as retail investors, we can't ignore this major thingamajig that's going on under our noses.

Also, we need to know and understand that a stock may trade differently around its dividend period.

People may be buying the stock so they can claim its dividend. Investors who are short the stock (have sold shares they do not own expecting the price to fall) may cover their positions (buy back the shares they have sold) so they don't have to pay the dividend. We need to understand that the share price will fall once the stock has gone ex-dividend. If we understand when dividends are being paid, it allows us to understand and account for share-price movement during the stock's dividend period.

The vast majority of dividends (especially in the United Kingdom) are ordinary dividends, meaning that you get paid what everybody else who owns an ordinary share gets paid. However, you may come across a preferred stock and a preferred dividend. If you do, you need to spend some time to really understand what you're buying. Preferred dividends are normally higher in price than ordinary dividends, but maybe the preferred shares don't have any voting rights at the AGM.

Another example from the FTSE 100 is Royal Dutch A or B shares. The only difference between the A and B shares is that the tax treatment in the Netherlands on the A shares is different from that on the B shares, so a UK investor would probably want to buy the B shares, which are cheaper. I have to be honest; 99 percent of stocks you look at will be nice and simple with one dividend, but I wanted to flag the possibility of preferred dividends. If you are thinking of buying shares with a preferred dividend, phone your broker and ask what the difference is.

### How does a dividend get paid?
### What's the timetable?

We also need to understand the mechanics behind dividends in terms of how we physically get paid. Your broker will normally do all this for you and will either send you a cheque or put the money into your share-trading account, or you may have decided to reinvest the dividend payment back into the company's shares. You do, however, need to understand the dividend process, related dates, and so forth. The typical dividend-payment timetable for a full-year dividend may look something like this:

Ex-Dividend Date (Normally a Wednesday in the United Kingdom)

Record Date (Normally a Friday in the United Kingdom and normally three days after the ex-dividend date)

AGM (Normally a few months after the ex-dividend date)

Payment Date (Normally a week or two after the AGM)

So what's the difference between all of the above dates, and are they important? The answer is that the ex-dividend date is the most important and one you should always know. You need to own shares in the company on the ex-dividend date in order to get the dividend. Shares pay their dividends before the market opens on the Wednesday morning, so you have to buy shares in the company by the close of markets on Tuesday evening if you want to receive the dividend.

The record date is always three days after the ex-dividend date, because settlement in the United Kingdom is three days. As you may know, when you sell shares, it takes your broker three days to send you your money back. This is because in the United Kingdom, it takes three days to transfer the money to the clearing house and for the clearing house to process your payment and transfer the shares into your name.

The AGM is normally a few months later, and generally this is a formality as shareholders vote to approve the dividend payment. I can't remember a single example of UK shareholders voting against the board of directors and refusing to allow them to pay a dividend, but I'm sure it has happened at some point in history. Assuming the AGM goes to plan and shareholders vote to accept the dividend, it's actually paid a week or two later. This is important. If you own a share on ex-dividend date, you don't actually get the cold hard cash for a few months, so you need to factor this in if you are going to become a dividend-loving investor.

> **Tip:** Share prices drop once they go ex-dividend.
>
> I am often asked if you should buy shares on the Tuesday night and sell them again on the Wednesday morning so that you receive the dividend but limit the amount of market exposure.
>
> Unfortunately, nothing is that easy, although there are many professional investors who try to do exactly that. The share will always open at a lower price on the ex-dividend date, roughly the same amount as the dividend. So if the company is paying a thirty-pence-per-share dividend, the shares will open down thirty pence on ex-dividend day.
>
> This is another reason retail investors need to know and understand dividends. Imagine if your stop-loss was triggered because a stock went ex-dividend, and you hadn't realized.

Just to follow that last point up, you may or may not hear the phrases "cum dividend" and "ex-dividend." I'm not sure why the market needs to randomly start using Latin in the middle of all this, but it has. Cum dividend is Latin for "with dividend," and, you guessed it, ex-dividend means it's trading without dividend. Any time between the ex-dividend date and the payment date, the stock is trading ex-dividend. At other times, it's trading cum dividend. I know we have already covered that, but I wanted to introduce market names in case you hear investors on CNBC or Bloomberg TV using them.

## Divided ratios

So I think that's about enough of general dividend chit-chat. Let's look at some cold hard ratios to help us decide if a stock is a good dividend payer or not. The good news is that this is all done for you, and the information you need is everywhere, so you won't have to look hard to find it. The market looks at three ratios: total dividends per share, dividend yield, and dividend cover. So let us jump in.

## Total dividends per share

This does exactly what it says on the tin. How much is each dividend worth on a per-share basis? You don't even need to work this out, as companies do it for you. A company may announce that they are returning £100 million to shareholders in the form of dividends, but this will nearly always be released with a friendly fifty pence per share. If they don't give you the total-dividends-per-share number, simply divide the total dividend payment by the number of shares outstanding.

The market uses total dividends per share because it's quite common for companies to pay a main final dividend once a year and also pay interim dividends at other times of the year. The final dividend usually relates to last year's profits, and the interim dividend usually relates to this year's profits. So total dividends per share is the total amount of dividends received (final and interim).

It's crucial for a retail investor to know how much dividend is being paid and when the ex-dividend dates are and to be prepared for stock-price moves around the ex-dividend dates.

## Dividend yield

We have established that receiving a dividend is almost like a second income, but we need to understand if a dividend is good or bad when compared against its share price. Is it worth paying a high share price to receive a good dividend, or not?

The simple way to look at this is to look at the dividend yield. Take Company X, for example. It's offering a full-year dividend of fifty pence per share (forty pence full-year and ten pence interim dividend). Its current share price is nine hundred pence per share. Divide the dividend by the current share price and multiply by one hundred.

$$\frac{Full\text{-}year\ dividend}{Current\ share\ price} \times 100 = Dividend\ yield$$

So to use the example above,

$$\frac{Full\text{-}year\ dividend = 50p}{Current\ share\ price = 900p} \times 100 = Dividend\ yield\ of\ 5.55\%$$

A dividend yield of 5.55 percent, but is that good or bad? The first thing you need to do is compare this company yield with that of other companies in the same sector to see how it compares against its competitors. You can even compare it against the FTSE 100 as a whole. You could compare 5.55 percent against investing in a bond where you don't have the risk of the company as a whole going bust or a director running away with all the money. You could consider comparing a 5.55 percent dividend yield against keeping your money in a high-interest savings account and not having any risk at all (unless the bankers are investing in more dodgy sub-prime stuff again).

So a dividend yield is a quick snapshot of the return you would get if you bought the shares at the current market price. It obviously does not take into account that the share price could also rise, and you could receive a capital gain as well (it could also fall, and you could make a loss).

But just how safe is the dividend? Is the company likely to pay a dividend next year and the year after that? Let's take a look at dividend cover.

### Dividend cover

We need to understand how much of the company's profits are being paid back to shareholders in dividends. The way we do this is by using our old friend EPS (earnings per share – remember step 2?). If a company has earnings per share of fifty pence, it could (in theory) pay a fifty-pence-per-share dividend. However, a company will never pay 100 percent of its profits in dividends. It will always keep some back for a rainy day. Dividend cover helps us understand how much they are paying out and keeping back.

$$\frac{EPS\ (earnings\ per\ share)}{DPS\ (dividend\ per\ share)} = Dividend\ cover$$

Let's look at Company X; it has EPS of fifty pence and proposes paying a dividend of ten pence.

$$\frac{EPS\ (earnings\ per\ share) = 50p}{DPS\ (dividends\ per\ share) = 10p} = Dividend\ cover\ 5X$$

To think of this another way, the company can pay the dividend five times before it starts to run out of profits. This shows us that a high dividend cover is great, as it gives us comfort that dividends will continue to be paid in the future (and maybe even increased). However the opposite is true, if you start to see dividend cover falling, it suggests that in future the company may not have enough spare cash to pay a dividend. Falling dividend cover can be an early warning sign that all is not right with the business, so it's definitely worth keeping an eye on!

### Debenhams versus Marks & Spencer

Let's compare our two general retailers on dividends.

|  | Div Per Share | Div Yield | Div Cover |
|---|---|---|---|
| Debenhams | 3.4p | 4.42% | 2.28x |
| Marks & Spencer | 18p | 3.45% | 1.97x |

It's much the same as the debt situation; the dividend paid by both of these companies is roughly the same. They both offer good dividend yields and are both at least two times covered (but Debenhams is actually nearer three times covered, so it offers an extra layer of safety).

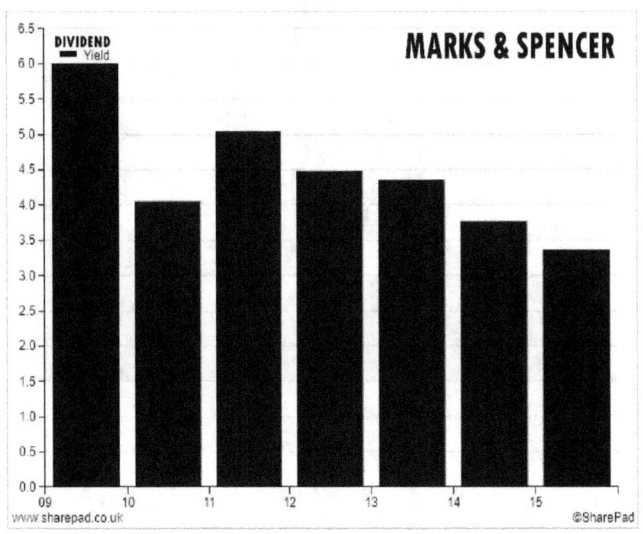

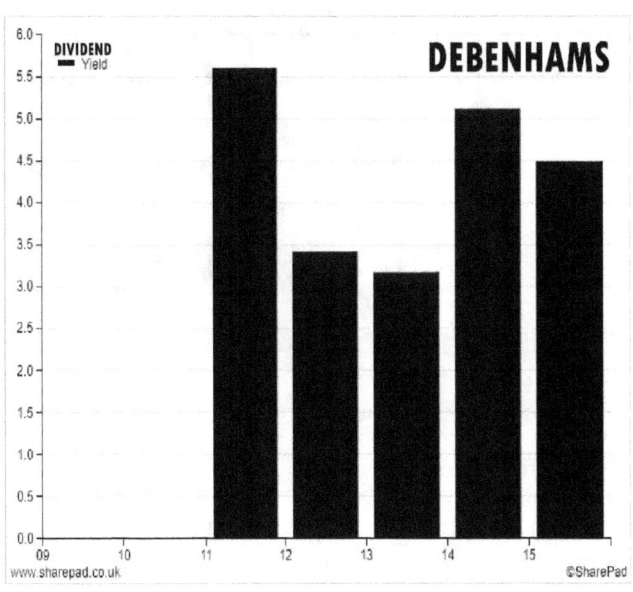

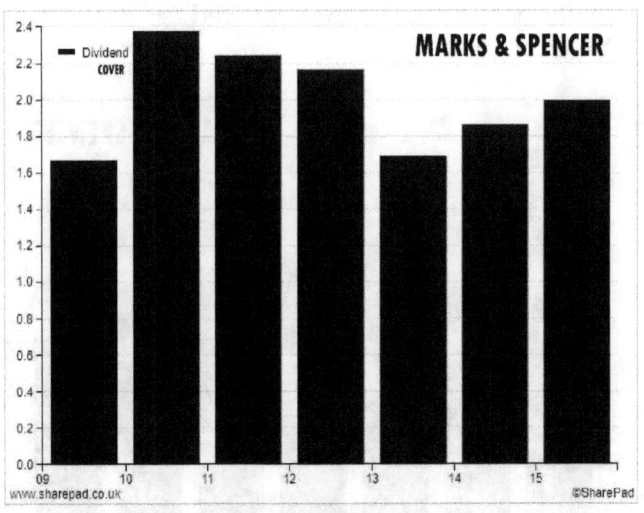

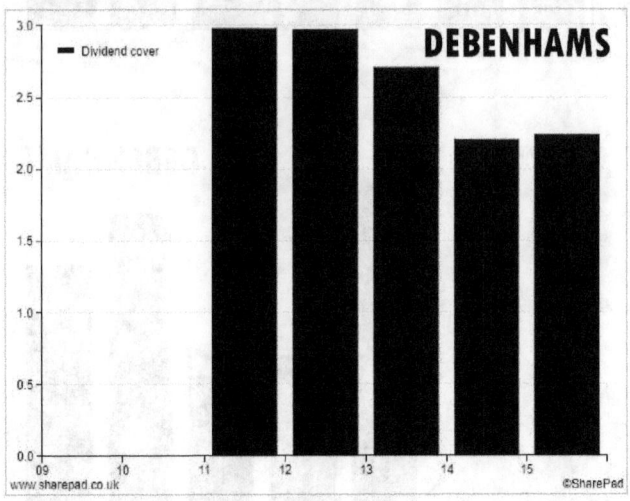

## Share buybacks

I love share buybacks. If you are looking for capital gains over dividends, focus on companies that are buying back their own shares. If a company buys its own shares, it's removing them from circulation. Therefore, the next time you work out the company's EPS, you are dividing earnings by fewer shares. This will improve the P/E ratio and so on.

As long as company earnings remain the same, the share price will go higher. If you can find an under-valued company with regular earnings growth that is buying back its own shares, this is a huge tick in my book.

## Key points from step 8

- How important are dividends to you? Are you looking for guaranteed dividends to add income, or are they just a bonus?

- Would you prefer to invest in a company that buys back its own shares or one that pays a dividend?

- Learn the dividend-payment calendar, and don't get caught out by ex-dividend dates and pay dates.

- Stocks fall following a dividend payment; don't get caught out with stop-losses.

- Dividend per share tells you how much divi-dend you receive per share you own.

- Dividend yield tells you in percentage terms how much divided you receive versus the dividend share price. It allows you to quick-ly compare how much dividend you get from one stock to another. The higher the yield, the better.

- Divided cover tells you how many times the company could pay the dividend. The low-er the number, the more risk the dividend could get cancelled; the higher the number, the safer the divided.

- Look at historic dividend payments, and understand if the dividend is rising or falling. A falling dividend could spell trouble ahead.

Just some final thoughts about dividends. A dividend is not just a source of income; it is a window directly into the heart of the company. What a dividend can tell you about a business is priceless. If a company's dividend is raised each year, this is a good sign that profits are rising year on year. Alternatively, if dividends are cut or cancelled, this is a huge indication that not all is well and that there could be trouble ahead. But while there's music and moonlight and love and romance, let's face the music and dance. (Sorry, I got carried away.)

As well as looking at dividend per share, dividend yield, and dividend cover, you need to look at historic payments and understand if dividend payments are consistent and growing, or inconsistent and falling.

# Step 9:

# Return on Equity (ROE), Return on Capital Employed (ROCE) and Free Cash Flow (FCF)

The last ratio, I promise. We are nearly finished, so please hang in there. ROCE is a great ratio, and you need it in your investor's toolbox. If you are a Warren Buffett fan, one of his golden rules is that a company should have high ROCE and low debt, and if it does, he is interested.

### Return on Equity (ROE)

To understand return on capital employed (ROCE), you need to understand return on equity (ROE). ROE simply looks at the relationship between earnings and shareholder equity. For example, Company X makes profits of £50 million, but its shareholder equity is £250 million. Divide £50 million by £250 million, and you get a return of 20 percent. In theory, that sounds amazing. A 20 percent return makes you want to sit up and take notice straight away.

$$\frac{\text{Earnings (or profits)}}{\text{Shareholder equity}} = \text{ROE}$$

To use the Company X example above,

$$\frac{\text{£50m earnings}}{\text{£250m shareholder equity}} = 20\% \text{ ROE}$$

As you can see, this is a fairly useful guide, but it doesn't include any debt calculations. We need a ratio that looks at ROE but takes it a stage further, and that will be ROCE.

> **Tip:** Think of return on equity like buying a buy-to-let house. Which of the following two houses would you chose to buy?
>
> House A costs £100,000, and you would receive £1000 rent each month.
>
> House B costs £100,000, and you would receive £750 rent each month.
>
> Hopefully you would agree that House A offers a better return on your equity investment.

## Return on capital employed (ROCE)

ROCE does not look at just earnings or profits. It looks at net operating profit after tax. This means we look at the profit the company would make if it did not have to pay any interest on its debt.

Also, ROCE does not just look at shareholder equity. It also looks at the total capital employed, which is shareholder equity plus debt.

Let's assume that Company X from the example above pays £10 million in interest each year and has £250 million in debt. Its profits are now £60 million, divided by total capital employed, which is £500 million. So Company X's ROCE is 12 percent. This is a lot less attractive than the 20 percent ROE figure, but it is a lot more representative of the per-pound return invested in assets within the business.

$$\frac{\text{Net operating profits after tax (before interest)}}{\text{Total capital employed}} = \text{ROCE}$$

Based on the example above,

$$\frac{\text{£60m net operating profits after tax (before interest)}}{\text{£500 m total capital employed (debt + shareholder equity)}} = \text{ROCE of 12\%}$$

If you are struggling with the maths and getting confused with net profits after tax and before interest and so forth, don't worry. You don't have to do the maths. The ROCE figure is widely published and quoted by journalists all the time. You just need to understand that this ratio measures the return (profit) per pound invested in assets within the business. On this basis, the higher the ROCE, the better. If you are really struggling with ROCE and don't know what I am talking about, the most crude and basic way I can explain it is that if you put money into the business (buy shares), the ROCE gives you a basic guide to what you can expect to get out if the business does not fundamentally change its costs or profits.

**Compare ROCE with competitors and stocks in the same sector and index**

Again, you need to compare ROCE only against stocks in the same sector. Also, I should just flag that I have used the most common way of working out ROCE. Some analysts use slightly different profit and capital-employed numbers, so only use the ROCE figures from the same provider (don't use the ROCE figure for one business from one website, and the other company's ROCE figure from a completely unrelated newspaper or magazine).

## Can you trust ROCE?

Critics of ROCE draw attention to its weaknesses. They rightly point out that ROCE is out of date as soon as you calculate it, as it uses numbers from an out-of-date balance sheet. Also, ROCE gives you no idea of the size of a company. You should think about investing in a company with a market cap of £50 million differently than investing in a company with a £500 million market cap, but ROCE does not take this into account.

I agree that ROCE has its weaknesses, but so does every single ratio out there. There is no perfect ratio. If there were, everybody would use it, and every-body would be rich. ROCE is a tool for your toolbox and should be used in combination with all the others we have talked about.

## Introducing Free Cash Flow

The final thing you need to look at before we move onto phase 2, but its an important one so please stay with me. You need to understand that cash flow and profit are completely different things.

A car company makes a profit when it sells a car for a higher price than it cost to manufacture that car. The business technically makes that profit at the moment it sells the car, but it may not receive the actual cash for weeks, months or years afterwards. It will report that car sale as profit, but it may not actually have the money.

To go a step further, a business can survive for years, buying raw materials on credit, selling its goods on credit, making profits but never actually having cash in their bank account. At any moment this could go horribly wrong. For this reason we need to run a fi-nal check on our investments, and make sure that they are converting their profits into cold hard cash. If they are not, or the company is struggles for cash, Huston we may have a problem.

Free cash flow is the term given to the cash that's left after a company has paid all its bills. A good company will be good at converting its profits into cashflow, and poor company will struggle to do so.

This is another incredibly complex subject and enough to scare a lot of retail investors off. If you are one of them, just please type into Google you company name and free cash flow and see what comes up. If you are met with hundreds of news stories highlighting problems, avoid investing.

If you don't have access to a wizzy website that will tell you the number, you can find the Free Cash Flow (FCF) number in the company accounts. Compare the FCF number to total sales and that will give you a good idea how much profit the company is converting into cash.

Once you become an advanced investor, you can learn a lot by analysing a companies FCF. However as I promised to keep things as easy as I could for now, I just want you to be aware of FCF and make sure your chosen investment is not struggling to convert its profits into cash!

## Marks & Spencer vs Debenhams

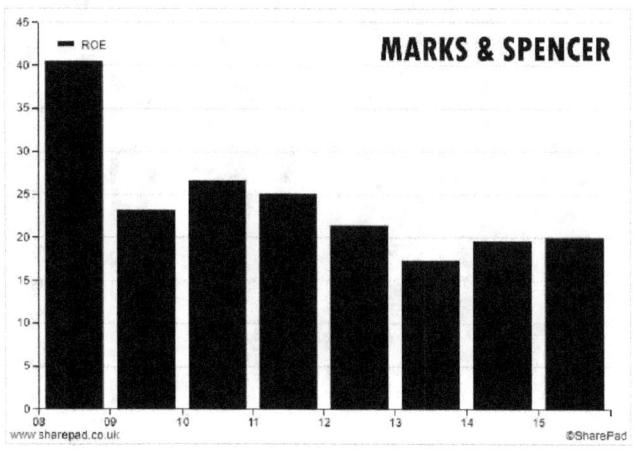

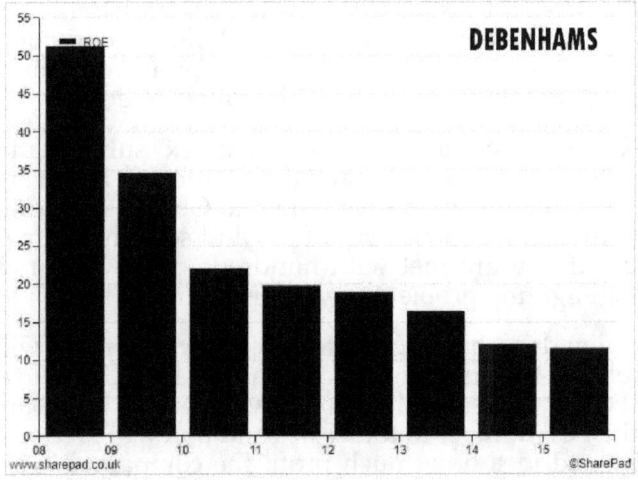

As you can see from the ROE charts above, both Marks & Spencer and Debenhams' ROE is in decline, admittedly Debenhams is a more rapid and consistent decline. I would go as far to say that Debenhams is exactly what you are looking for, just in the opposite direction!

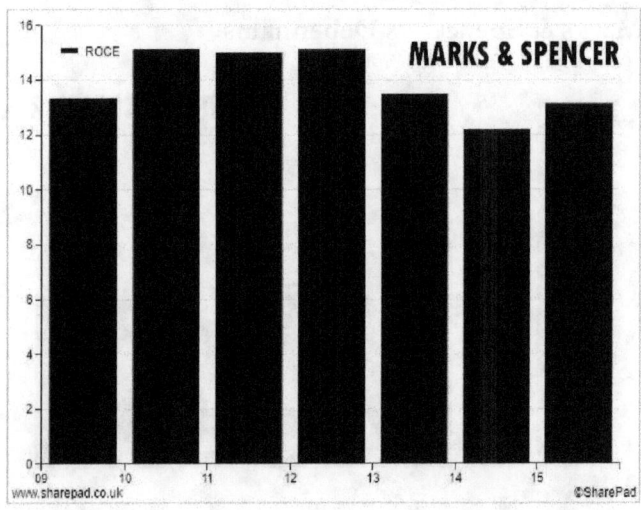

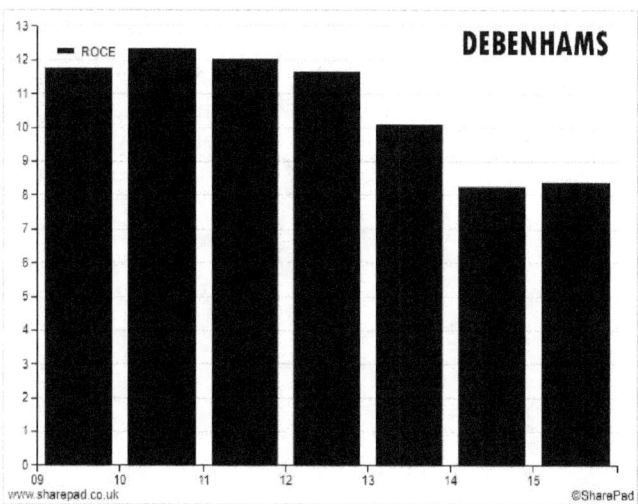

Again the ROCE graphs tell the story. Both companies ROCE is low and falling. We want high and rising!

**Key points from step 9**

- We want to buy a good company at the right time, and ROCE is a key ratio to help us understand if it's a good company or not.

- If you invest capital into a business, you want the return on that capital to be as high as possible.

- We are looking for companies with a high ROCE.

- Warren Buffett stresses that a high ROCE and low debt is critical, or he will refuse to invest.

- Make sure your investment is good at converting its profits into cash. Remember cash and profits are totally different things.

So that's it, the end of phase 1. Let's regroup and refresh and move on to phase 2, which is a lot more fun! But first, let's look back at everything we have learned during phase 1 and draw up some conclusions!

# Conclusion to Phase 1

So that's it, the end to the quantitative stage (or, in English, an end to all the boring ratios and mathematics). I am hoping that you're buzzing with excitement, because you should now be able to look at the fundamental-research section of any share and at a snapshot understand whether it is undervalued or overvalued in relation to its current share price. Remember the table from the introduction? You are now able to understand what the vast majority of the items on that table are telling you.

Most importantly, you are now able to look at the data and decide in three or four minutes if a share is worth spending more time on or not. Phase 1 on its own cannot tell you enough information about a share to decide if you should buy it, but it can tell you enough to know not to buy it.

When I do seminars, I am nearly always asked why I don't use the inventory-turnover ratio, or the net-sales-to-working capital ratio, or how I can sleep at night without looking a Z score. There are millions of ratios I don't use, and I don't understand half of them. That's not to say they are beyond comprehension, as most ratios are simple to understand once you spend time looking at them. But at some point, you have to say enough is enough. We are retail investors, we don't have the time and resources to research everything in detail. The ratios I have given you will give you a solid base to work from.

If you have a favourite ratio you know and understand — perfect, add it to the mix. If you are a trained accountant and can cross-examine the balance sheet in the annual report — again, do it! I am not telling you to forget all the other ratios and financial info out there; it's all important, and please add all your extra knowledge into the process. However, if you picked up this book with little knowledge of how to value a stock, phase 1 gives you a really good, basic understanding.

If I were still a professional investor or writing a book for professional investors, I would add more ratios to strengthen phase 1, but we are retail investors, and we don't have the time. We could easily spend all our time doing analysis and none of our time investing. What we have looked at during phase 1 is the market norm, and it gives us a general overview of what's happened to a company in the past and, to a certain extent, the present. Following the ratios in phase one also means you still have time to do the day job, look after the kids, take the dog for a walk and cut the back lawn. It's a realistic attempt to furnish retail investors with solid information which won't take up loads of your time!

You will notice that, with the exception of the PEG ratio in step 6, we have not looked into the future. That's because that's what phase 2 is all about. The simple truth is that there are few reliable and accurate ways to look at the future of a share price. Retail investors who live in the real world and have a good understanding of the businesses they are buying are just as likely to correctly predict the future as professional investors who live and work in the cocoon of central London and live their lives with no comprehension of what's happening in the industrial north of England.

Now that you have learned phase 1 and know about EPS, P/E ratio, price-to-book ratios, EV/EBITDA, PEG, company debt, and dividends, you have learned a lifelong skill. These were the same valuation methods used in the 1980s, and they will still be used in 2030. Sure, a clever analyst will come out and claim a P/E isn't any good and we should use something else, and that could be true, but you can trust and continue to use the fundamental skills we learned in phase 1 to give you a snapshot of the current value of a company.

Remember our Debenhams versus Marks & Spencer comparison? Take a look at the same data below, and you should now be able to understand what is what!

| Debenhams Key Numbers | | | |
|---|---|---|---|
| Latest Share Price (P) | 76.73 | Net Gearing % | 58.65 |
| Market Capitalisation (m) | 944.85 | Gross Gearing % | 60.18 |
| Shares in Issue (m) | 1227.08 | Debt Ratio | 41.03 |
| P/E Ratio | 10.13 | Debt-to-Equity Ratio | 0.46 |
| Total dividends per share (p) | 3.4 | Assets / Equity Ratio | 2.51 |
| Dividend Yield (%) | 4.42 | Cash / Equity Ratio | 3.83 |
| Dividend Cover (x) | 2.28 | Price to book value | 1.11 |
| NAV per share (p) | 0 | ROCE | 7.84 |
| Earnings per share (p) | 7.6 | EPS Growth (%) | 7.04 |
| 52 week high / low | 96.35 / 63.75 | DPS Growth (%) | 0 |

| Marks & Spencer Key Numbers | | | |
|---|---|---|---|
| Latest Share Price (P) | 409.45 | Net Gearing % | 58.46 |
| Market Capitalisation (m) | 6764.47 | Gross Gearing % | 60.97 |
| Shares in Issue (m) | 1648.26 | Debt Ratio | 47.43 |
| P/E Ratio | 13.82 | Debt-to-Equity Ratio | 0.58 |
| Total dividends per share (p) | 18.00 | Assets / Equity Ratio | 2.56 |
| Dividend Yield (%) | 3.45 | Cash / Equity Ratio | 6.44 |
| Dividend Cover (x) | 1.97 | Price to book value | 2.66 |
| NAV per share (p) | 0.00 | ROCE | 9.86 |
| Earnings per share (p) | 29.5 | EPS Growth (%) | -8.62 |
| 52 week high / low | 600.00 / 694.60 | DPS Growth (%) | 5.88 |

See what I did there? You actually do know what most of these are. We have used the majority of the above numbers in steps 1 to 9.

So how should you use the information you can now extract from phase 1? You should use it as a guide only. You need more information in order to buy a share. You need to understand the company's aims and future direction; you need to look at the management and decide if they have it in them to achieve this growth. You need to extract any information you can about possible future earnings, and most importantly, you need to remain objective and open minded. At this point, we need to use the results from phase 1 to decide if we are going to bother with the significant amount of work ahead or not.

It's up to you where you get your financial data from. In a perfect world, I would ask you to do all the work yourself. Head to the company's latest annual report and work out the profit and debt ratios for yourself, as this is the only way to be 100 percent sure you are looking at live, current, and reliable data. However, we live in the real world; you probably don't have time to do that because the cat has just been sick on the sofa, and you still need to paint the hallway! It's OK to use the Internet, a newspaper, or your broker for the financial data, but please be consistent. It's no good doing research using a newspaper one day, and your broker's data the next. Even if you use a source of information that is slow to update, at least be consistent so all your research is using the same (slow) information.

So what about Marks & Spencer vs. Debenhams? Which one should you buy? I have to be honest; at this stage I am failing to get excited about either of them. They are both doing OK, and they are profitable with controllable debt. They pay dividends, so there are worse companies out there. But I am struggling to be jumping up and down with excitement about owning either of them.

Marks is probably the better bet; it's making higher more consistent profits and has a stronger ROCE. However, its historic EPS growth is rubbish at its PE at almost 14x earnings is again just about OK but hardly exciting. At this stage I would probably not bother looking any further into Marks, but the book can't end there, so let's continue. I would now go into stage two and look at Marks in more detail, and decide if there is something in the pipeline that's really exciting and makes Marks's value start to look cheap. If we can't find anything, then we should probably pass on this opportunity and go and look for something better!

And that, ladies and gentlemen, was my goal for phase 1! If you are now able to analyse a company in five minutes and work out if the stock is under-valued or overvalued in relation to its competitors, my aims have been achieved! Phase 1 is all about deciding if you want to bother looking in more de-tail or not.

If you want to research the investment in more de-tail, move on to phase 2 and spend as long as it takes looking into your possible investment. Phase 1 is about not investing loads of time researching a dud. Phase 2 is about saving and making you money. On that note, let's crack on.

# PHASE 2

# Step 10:

# Check the Company's Website and Most Recent Financial Reports

According to SEC research conducted in 2008 (sorry, this is the most up-to-date information I could find), only 3 percent of American retail investors use a company's annual report as a main source of investment information. In addition, only 6 percent will look at a company's website during the investment process. Although this research is eight years old and based on American retail investors, I think these numbers are roughly in line with how many UK retail investors currently look at the same information.

I know this sounds obvious, but you have to check the information the company gives you directly. It's amazing how few retail investors visit a company website or look at the annual report before they invest. Spend time getting to know the company via their websites and annual reports.

## Company website

Often a company will regularly update its website (more often than its annual report), and you can often pick up some great hints and tips for how the business is performing. The first thing I should flag is that companies often have two websites, one for consumers (the general public) and one for investors. You really need to spend a lot of time on both.

The first thing to do is use the website to gain a real and total understanding for what the business does. I am not talking about just the main stuff it does, but also all the other stuff as well. Take Pets at Home, for example. Everybody probably already knows it sells pet food and other related pet equipment, but by looking at the company website, you'll see that it also offers pet insurance, an in-house vet at every store, and an in-house grooming shop at each store (so you can take your dog for a haircut and bubble bath).

It also offers a range of services including microchip implanting, pet-nutrition consultations, flea-and-worm consultation, and many more expansions to their business. All this activity comes under "revenues" in the profit-and-loss account, so you need to know every little part of the business.

If it's a retail site, pretend you're a retail customer and shop around. See what it's like to use the website. Is it easy to navigate, and is it easy to find and buy the products? If it's not, would you (or do you already) use a competitor's website instead? Take Tesco, for example. Everybody knows what Tesco does; it's a supermarket. But look at the website, and you'll be pointed towards Tesco Express, an online supermarket where you can buy everything from table-tennis tables, robots (yes, a table-tennis robot), and other table-tennis equipment to kitchen dishwashers. There's even a section where you can preorder the latest John Grisham book. Is this a brilliant strategy to leverage their supermarket business to try to become the next Amazon, or is Tesco too late and lost its first-mover advantage? Have a good look at the Tesco Bank pages on the website, another major diversification away from the simple world of supermarkets and product margins and so forth. By spending time looking at the website, you can get a real feeling and understanding of a business and where it's moving to in the future.

If a company is spending a lot of effort pushing visitors away from its core business into other areas, maybe it's worried about the core business and sees the growth coming from other areas. That's OK, but if 95 percent of revenue comes from the core business, an investor could have a few rough years ahead. (Combine this idea with the ratios we looked at during phase 1. Falling EPS, falling dividends, and rising debts may support this theory.) On the flip side, maybe the core business is absolutely sound, and company management should be congratulated for not resting on their laurels and trying to abstract more growth from the business. (Rising EPS and rising dividend payments may support this argument.)

The last example is Thomas Cook, the travel company. On the website, you'll see a load of information about holidays and latest travel destinations. Take a look at a section called "Travel Updates." There's a long list of travel issues, including problems with holidays to Sharm El Sheikh in Egypt and Tunisia (judging by the holidays on sale elsewhere on the website, these are two major winter sun destinations for the business). If I were going to buy Thomas Cook shares, I would use the website to understand each and every holiday venue offered and think about any future possible problems they may encounter.

You want to spend a lot of time on the websites' news pages and read each and every story there. This is what the company wants the world to know it is doing, so as investors, you should take note. If a company has announced a new product, take a look at it, understand it, and understand that it will change the company's outlook and future revenues. If the company announces a regulatory change, try to understand if this is a major problem for the company or not. Sometimes companies put links to recent TV or radio interviews of management. It may be worth listening to how management is coming across and what is being said.

We have a whole chapter (step 12) about company management, so I don't want to talk about it here, but often the company's investor website has pictures and bios of its management personnel. Spend some time flicking through these and getting to know the people you are trusting your money with.

By looking at the investor's website, you also get a huge insight into how the company treats investors. Does it contain loads and loads of easily accessible information? Or is it difficult to get the information you need to make investment decisions? Is the investor site kept up to date? How easy is it to use? I don't want to be negative, but if the information you need is difficult to find, is the company trying to hide it from you? (Or is it just a bad website design, which would also worry me, because if a company can't get its own website right, what else is it getting wrong?)

At the least, visit the financial calendar. This should give you the dates of interim and full-year reports. Some good ones will also give you dividend details like ex-date, pay date, and so forth.

Have a look at the company investor and advisor contacts, and you will see who audits the accounts and, most importantly, which investment banks advise it. We'll talk about analysts' reports and share-price targets later, but you'll see a strong link between investment banks that advise companies and, coincidently, give the buy recommendations and high stock prices.

Have a look at the jobs page of the website. If the company is going through a growth phase, it should be recruiting a lot of staff. If the company is going through a difficult phase and still advertising for lots of jobs, this could mean staff turnover is high, which means staff morale is low. Management could be positive about the business and the turnaround story, but the jobs section of the website is telling you something different.

The main thing you can get from the investor website is the company aims for the next few years. Companies normally don't hide away from their three or four main goals. These goals are normally on the website in a nice box or graphic. They may state something like "To continue growing by continuing our aggressive M&A strategy." That tells you they're going to buy more companies in the future, so that strong cash-to-equity ratio that caught your eye that you hoped would be spent increasing the dividend is about to get a hammering.

A company's website is a huge window into the heart of the business. It's a breathing, living organism that is a current reflection of the company you are thinking about buying. I meet so many retail investors who have never visited the websites of the companies they own shares in.

Obviously a company won't write on the website, "We are terrible; don't buy shares in us." They'll be as positive as possible at all times. However, it's still a great resource, and a company's website is updated more often than its annual report. This is another tool in your investing toolbox and is best used alongside your other tools.

By the time you have finished looking at the website, you should be able to describe in some detail what the company does and describe all its products, not just the main ones. You should also have a good feel for and understanding of the business and what makes it tick. You should understand how it treats its investors and be able to extract some key information you need (like key dates, for example).

One last test you can do is send the company an e-mail or call the company phone number and ask to speak to investor relations. When and if you get through, say that you're a retail investor and are thinking about buying shares but have a question. Ask anything. Ask what staff turnover is like, or what percentage of business comes from the European Union and what percentage comes from the United Kingdom. It doesn't really matter what you ask them (although it helps if you actually have a question you would like to know the answer to). See how long this process takes and what response you get. If it's impossible to get through to investor relations and you are treated with contempt when you do, at least you know how they treat their investors, and you won't be surprised a few months later if they mislead you and issue a surprise profit warning.

## Company reports

A listed company has to (by law) release an annual report and an annual set of figures that have been audited by an independent accountant. If you are seriously thinking of investing in a company, you have to find its most recent annual report. (It's always found on the company's website.)

There are a few key sections you need to look at. At the front, there is always a statement from the CEO or chairman. Then there are normally reports from the key heads of each product or division. Towards the end, there is a section about directors and managers and how they get paid (we will cover this in step 12). Carry on flicking, and you'll find a section called risk and uncertainties. We need to have a look at this section. Normally at the back (just before the notes), there are the three sets of financial data the company is forced to release (profit-and-loss statement, income statement, and balance sheet).

We'll never be able to analyse a full-year report in the

same way as the professionals, and if the company is really motivated to bury bad news, they will find a way. (For your information, some analysts claim the bad news is always buried in the notes at the back, and they believe you should always start reading an annual report on the back page and read forward). However, we can't invest without looking at some major clues that the annual report can give us.

**Tip:** Call into or watch "research calls" or "earnings calls." When all companies release their annual reports, and when some of the larger companies release their trading updates, they also organise what's called an earnings "conference call" or more commonly nowadays a webinar.

This involves the company's management giving a presentation about their earnings and the current and future state of their business. Almost all key institutional investors and almost all investment-bank analysts who cover the stock from around the world will listen to this call (so there is a lot of technical jargon), and they are able to ask questions after the presentation.

If it's a really juicy call, the Q&A session can be intriguing. I have known these calls to go on for four hours or more if the company is in a mess or there is a special situation! These calls are a magnificent window into the business and what the professional investors think about it. You get the same info at the same time as the professional fund manager who owns 1 percent of the company.

As a retail investor, you are able to gain access to this call or webinar, but they probably won't let you ask a question unless it's a really small company without many analysts covering the stock. You can normally sign up via the company's website on the day the results are released. If you sign up, they normally will also give you access to a recording for up to forty-eight hours after the live event.

## Statement from the chairman or CEO

Within this document (usually at the front), there will be a statement from the chairman or CEO. It's crucial that you read this statement, as it will give you an overview of the business, where it has come from, where it currently is, and where it is going. This message is directly from the horse's mouth and is written specifically for investors, so why would you not want to read it? This message has not been interpreted by journalists or analysts. It's directly from the person running the company in which you are about to invest your hard-earned savings.

I agree that this message will be ultra-positive and won't be too self-critical, but it's also an insight into the future direction the company is going in and what the priorities are. If there is a fundamental change in policy (for example, they are going to look at mergers and acquisitions next year to boost growth), you really can't complain if the company buys another business a few months after you invest and the deal hits the share price.

They often mention new markets, new products, and new opportunities in this section, and you need to understand if the business is changing direction or diversifying. This is absolutely crucial. It's no good buying a company with great historic EPS growth and dividend cover if the company is changing direction and changing the business plan.

**Tip:** I accept that it can be boring reading all the different reports. There is a way you can cheat.

There are some words that are far more interesting than others, and these stand out when you read about companies and share prices. Words like *unexpected, difficult trading, below expectations, unpredictable,* or *challenging,* or maybe words like *transformational, exceeding expectations,* or *increased profit.* I'm sure you can come up with some of your own depending on what type of information you are looking for.

If you use Microsoft Word on your computer, when you get the report, copy and paste it into Word and run a "word finder" search on the document. You can then quickly jump into sections with your keywords in them.

You still end up doing a lot of reading, but at least it will be relevant stuff and not waffle.

## Risks and uncertainties section

In every annual report, there will also be a section called "Risks and Uncertainties" (or something similar). Before you invest, you absolutely have to find this section and read it. Read it in a cold, bright room and while you are standing up so your focus is 100 percent.

It's in this section that the company's management will highlight all the risks they can see for the business moving forward. As a retail investor, you don't need to do a load of work on the possible risks to the business. They do it for you. Find this section, read it, and make sure you are 100 percent comfortable with everything they are telling you.

Please remember that everybody does this, so don't be put off investing by reading this list. If all the risks are general "could happen to any company" types of risks, that's OK, and don't stress. If the risk is company-specific and sounds serious, you need to worry. For example, if the company lists things like a huge debt repayment is due next year and they don't have the working capital to pay for it, start running.

## Directors' pay and remuneration section

This section shows how much each director is paid and how they are paid. It's important to know if directors receive cash or shares as part of their salary, bonus, and pension schemes. I will go into this in more detail in step 12, so hold on for now.

## Balance sheet

As Thomas Ittelson put it, "What you own minus what you owe is what you are worth." That's exactly what a company balance sheet is. It's a list of everything the company owns (assets) and a list of everything the company owes (liabilities) and what it's worth (equity) on a single day in its recent history. You could look at a balance sheet as a formula if you wanted to.

> Assets (Own) - Liabilities (Owe) =
>
> Shareholders Equity (Worth)

The assets are listed at the top, and the liabilities are listed at the bottom. At the bottom of the balance sheet is an equity section that basically tells you where the money is coming from to fund any gaps between assets and liabilities. The current year's figures are on the left, and the previous year's figures are on the right. I won't go through every line on the balance sheet and explain each item one by one, but there are general themes we can quickly identify.

Without going into too much detail, you want to compare last year's figures with this year's and see if there are any stand-out improvements or deteriorations. From a balance sheet, you can see any dramatic changes to assets or liabilities that you might need to research further.

In the debt section, you can also see short-term liabilities (debt that needs to be paid back soon) and long-term liabilities (debt that can be paid back over the longer term). You need to be concerned if the short-term liabilities are significantly large.

I also get suspicious if there is a sudden, huge jump in intangible assets. These are assets like brand, customer loyalty, patents, and trademarks. It's difficult to quantify how much a brand is worth, so I always get concerned if there is a sudden, unexplained huge jump in intangible assets on the balance sheet.

Let's take Sam, for example, our football- and curry-loving friend from Sheffield. He goes on holiday each year to Norway with his friends, by the way. That's not specifically relevant, but I thought it was interesting. You could list all Sam's assets like his house, car, cash in the bank, stamp collection, and furniture under assets on his balance sheet. Under long-term liabilities, you could list his mortgage and car repayments, as they both have to be repaid over the next few years. Under short-term liabilities, you could list his credit-card debt and the £200 he borrowed from his mom and dad, because both need to be paid off in the next three months. So Sam's equity is all his assets minus all his debts. These need to balance in order for it to be an accurate balance sheet. By comparing last year's figures with this year's, we can see whether Sam's assets are rising or falling, whether his debts are rising or falling, and whether his overall equity is rising or falling.

## The income statement

The income statement is really interesting for investors because it shows how much of its products a company has sold (sales or revenue), how much a company has spent (costs), and how much money was left over (net income or profits or earnings) over the last twelve months.

Sales - Costs = Net Income

Many investors think this is the single-most important factor to look at and will only invest in companies with already strong and dramatically improving income statements.

Again, you can compare the current year with previous years to see if there are any dramatic jumps in sales, costs, or net income. If sales are rising, you should also expect to see costs rise roughly in-line.

If you are buying a company that has been making a loss for a long time, you need to see a progressive reduction in the loss year on year. If you are buying a stock for a turnaround story (a company that's been performing badly, and you think it will get better), this report will give you a pretty good idea of how close to profitability the company is.

## The cash-flow statement

The cash-flow statement shows the movement of cash in a company, so basically, it shows where the company gets its cash from and where it spends it. Anybody who runs a small business will tell you that cash flow and income are two completely separate things. You may make a product for £20,000 and sell it for £100,000, making £80,000 in profit, which looks great on the income statement. But if you aren't getting paid that £80,000 until the following year, your actual bank account just has the £20,000 of costs in it.

The cash-flow statement is crucial, because profitable companies can struggle with cash-flow issues. A cash-flow statement looks at the company's ability to pay its bills.

Again, we can't go into too much detail, but you are looking for significant changes from last year to this year.

## Last thoughts about looking at the annual report

I have flown through the income statement, balance sheet, and cash-flow statement, as I assume you aren't an accountant. If you are, or if you have basic accountancy knowledge, I strongly recommend you spend more time looking at these crucial documents and learning about them. However, I am on a mission to make investing as easy as possible for the retail investor.

For the typical retail investor with no accountancy experience, I am going to ask you to glance at the balance sheet and income and cash-flow statements to pick up any significant changes from year to year. Look at the risks the company is worried about, and read the chairman's statement at the beginning.

## Prospectus or Admission Document

If your chosen company is new or very young or in the process of offering new shares, you may be able to get hold of the company prospectus. If you can, they are well worth flicking through.

If a company intends to list on the stock exchange for the first time or plans to issue new shares, it must issue a prospectus that is packed full of information about the company, its sector, and its future direction. These can be difficult to get hold of as they are sent to institutional shareholders, but you can usually find them on the company's website.

Smaller companies that are listing on the stock exchange for the first time don't always have to publish a huge, glossy, full-colour prospectus, but they do have to complete and publish an admission document. Again, these are packed full of useful information.

It's worth keeping an eye out for any for these documents, but as always remember these are gloss sales documents always putting the company in the best light possible. It's like looking at new houses on a website; they will take pictures of the house on a beautiful sunny day, and everything will be tidy and bright and will look idyllic. It's only when you visit the house you realize it backs onto a motorway; is directly under the flight path; and is next door to a noisy, smelly, glue-making factory.

## Investor Presentations

Occasionally a company will issue an investor presentation. If you are a shareholder, there is a tiny chance you may get an invite, but these are normally attended by the professionals only. Companies may hold or publish an investor presentation when something interesting is going on (good or bad). Sometimes if the company has a new product, or is changing direction, or has identified an opportunity, the company may issue a presentation about current market conditions or a change in a major raw material they use. Whatever the reason for giving an investor presentation, it's usually followed (directly or indirectly) by the company asking for more money.

Keep an eye out for investor presentations. They can tell you a huge amount about the business.

## Key points from step 10

- The company website and annual report are critical resources rarely used by retail investors.

- A company website lets you understand exactly what products and services the company is selling and where their focus is.

- A chairman's report at the front of an annual report gives a biased but useful overview of where the company is and where it's trying to get to.

- Make sure you read the risks and uncertainties section of the annual report; you may find all sorts of risks you had not considered.

- Contact the company and ask a question; you will they get an understanding of how they treat retail investors.

- Sign up for the earnings call that goes alongside the annual earnings report, and listen in or watch.

- If you know how to read company accounts, spend a long time looking at the annual accounts (balance sheet, income statement, and cash-flow statement). If you don't know how to read them, just glance over the accounts and look for any significant jumps or falls. Send off an e-mail to the investor-relations department asking what the big jump or fall is about.

- Keep an eye out for investor presentations or a company prospectus or admission documents. All are important pieces of info about the company.

Now that we know what the company is saying about itself and we know all about its products and services, we need to look at what everybody else is saying about the company. I call the next step the company background check. Remember that a company will always portray itself in the best light possible, so we need other peoples' opinions.

# Step 11:
# Company Background Check

This step involves obtaining as much information about the company as you can and involves a lot of surfing the web (which will please some of you but horrify others). Your mindset at this point is really important. You may be thinking that you have found a great share, and you just want to get on and buy it. Get into the mindset of trying to find reasons to not buy the share, rather than looking for more positive reinforcement as to why you should buy it.

## YouTube

The first place I always start is with YouTube. Did you know that YouTube is the world's second-largest search engine and it's owned by Google, the world's largest search engine? Type the company name into YouTube, and see what you get. If it's a small company, you may draw a blank, but you will likely be amazed by what you can find. The director of the company may have been interviewed at some business convention in Las Vegas, and somebody has posted it online. I love to try to find the directors out of their natural habitats talking about business. You can often get crucial insights.

You may also find all sorts of weird and wonderful stuff, some of which can be useful. You will probably find all the company's old TV advertisements, which won't really help you. However, I have found internal company training videos as well as snippets of documentaries and TV shows about the company I am interested in. You may find footage of the company's Christmas party or the management at an awards ceremony. You may find all sorts of useful stuff, and even stuff that's not useful still helps you get in touch with the business and understand its brand and the people who work for it.

Once you have searched on YouTube for the company, do a general search about the sector it's in and see what comes up. You may find a stock analyst talking about the sector and about your company. Play with YouTube, and see what you can find. Hardly any professional investors use YouTube, and even fewer retail investors use it.

### News articles

By far the most important source of information is news articles. I go back and read all the news articles from about the last two years. This gives you a unique insight into the company and the business you won't get from looking at historic EPS ratios.

By reading the news stories, you might get a whole new insight into the business. For example, a company's financial ratios, dividends, and debt might all be perfect, and the company website looks amazing, but when you start reading news stories, you suddenly realize that all the journalists are talking about is the government changing the regulations next year, which will impact the company's earnings. Maybe the journalists talk about two rival companies that are growing aggressively and taking market share from the company you are interested in.

As a retail investor, you are not alone. You don't need to do all the work and analysis by yourself. There are financial websites that do all the financial ratios for you. There are news websites that do all the background checks and "digging for dirt" for you, so make sure you use them.

It's worth looking at news websites, but it's also worth checking Google in two different ways. Type the company's name into Google and then click on the news tab and go through about two years of news stories; however, it's also worth looking at the main Google search engine as well. (Please note that I am not recommending Google; other search engines are available.)

## Search engines like Google

The main search engine will have loads of results for your company, so make sure you go past page 1. I go back to about page 30 of Google and read every little tinpot website's opinion on the stock. This will be boring, but you'll occasionally find something, and it will be like a light bulb going off in your head. You'll suddenly stop what you're doing and decide not to buy.

In my experience, the most interesting information I find is never directly about the stock I'm interested in; it's about a competitor or rival. Sometimes it's an industry or government report, but it makes you think, "Hold on a minute."

You also need to search if your company has one large client—for example, a medical supplier that has 90 percent of its revenue from the National Health Service. One is the most dangerous number in business (one client, one staff member, one supplier, etc.). If a business has one major client, you should be seriously worried anyway, but you also want to do a news search and a general Internet search about that one client as well.

## Customer reviews

During your company background check, you should also be looking at reviews the general public has written about the company. I know nobody spends the time to write a good review, and everybody spends the time to write a bad review, but it's still a good guide for how the business is performing. For example, if you come across a load of reviews from people complaining that they bought a product that was out of stock and took six weeks to deliver, it may indicate the business has a problem with manufacturing or distribution. Don't worry if it's one or two people having a general moan, but if it's lots of people, it can represent a problem.

Go as far as you can, and spend as much time investigating as you can. We are trying to pick up hints, tips, and news about the company that indicate its future performance. Financial ratios, dividends, and debt levels are important to inform you about past and present share-price valuations, but this company background check is more about real life. We are trying to build a picture about the future, and we're looking at competitor advantage, brand loyalty, company costs, geographical diversity, and all those other things ratios can't tell you.

### Key things you need to be looking out for

There are some key terms and phrases you need to be looking out for, like …

- "Profit warning"
- "Stronger than expected" or "Weaker than expected"
- "Merger", "Acquisition" or "Takeover"
- "Rights issue"
- "Stake-building"
- "Broker upgrade" or "Broker downgrade"

- "Pension fund deficit"

- "Sale and leaseback"

- "Investigation"

- "Resignation" or "sacking"

…and so on and so on. I am sure you will be able to add to this list drawing from past experiences you may have had. So for example, if I was researching Debenhams, I would go through the above list and type "Debenhams Profit Waring" in Google and see what comes up. I would then type "Debenhams stronger than expected" and see what comes up.

## Avoid confirmation bias

Confirmation bias is fundamentally the theory that once we have made a decision to buy something, then it's human nature to then only look for evidence to support that decision.

For example, if you are thinking of booking a summer holiday to Spain, you will have an open mind and will look at all evidence good and bad which will help make your decision. However once you have made your decision and booked the holiday, you will then only look for evidence that confirms that you've made the right decision. You will dismiss the negative reviews as people whinging, and will wholeheartedly agree with the positive reviews. This is human nature, and it's hard to fight against!

You must fight against confirmation bias when doing your company background check. If you really want to find positive news because sub-consciously you want to invest, you will find good news to reinforce your decision and you will dismiss the bad news which may have held you back.

I talk about confirmation bias again later in this book. However the concept of confirmation bias at this stage is crucial. You must keep an open mind when conducting your general company background check.

## Key points from step 11

- Do as much background research as you can.

- YouTube can be a gold mine of hidden videos and information.

- Check out customer reviews. If they are overwhelmingly bad, it may suggest a problem.

- Read historic news articles about the business.

- Do background research on the sector and competitors, in particular checks about new competitors or regulations changing the marketplace.

- Draw up a list of key words you will search for in Google and YouTube.

- Avoid confirmation bias!

While you're going through this stage, you'll find loads of information about directors' shareholdings and institutional shareholders. I will be talking a lot more about these in the next chapter (step 12), so on that note, let's get on with it.

# Step 12:

# Management Check, Directors' Dealings, Institutional Shareholders, and Short Interest

If you spend Sunday nights watching *Dragons' Den* on the BBC, you will have heard the dragons talking about investing in people as much as in the business itself. This is exactly the same as a retail investor investing in the stock market. A company's management can give you huge clues about if you should invest or not.

We need to be realistic. The average retail investor can't spend loads of time analysing the CVs of company management. I don't expect you to have a huge folder with the personal details of all the corporate movers and shakers of the business world.

However, if you are thinking of investing in a company, you should at least have a look at the names, photos, and brief biographies of the key people on the investor pages of the website. This will give you an immediate snapshot of who these people are, how long they have been directors, and what part they have played in building the business so far.

### Are the owners of the business invested?

There are no hard-and-fast rules regarding company management, but a number of top professional fund managers spend hours researching company management. What they are looking for are directors who are shareholders or owners of the business.

This makes perfect sense when you stop to think about it. When the people who run the company you are thinking of investing in get paid a small salary but receive a large number of shares in the business, they are motivated to make sure the business and the share price perform well. On the flip side, people who earn £5 million a year wages and have no shares in the business are probably more motivated to look after themselves than to worry about the share price. This is a sweeping generalization, and you may think I'm being unfair, but it's something you should look at.

You would also hope that the company's management is not stupid. If they are happy to be paid in shares, they at least believe in the long-term future of the business. Would you take a job and be paid in shares if you thought the company was doomed and the future was bleak?

Going back to Warren Buffett and his golden rules of investing, he always asks if the management are owners of the business. Are they invested? He is one of those fund managers who like company management to be in the same boat they are in (i.e., their financial futures are linked to the success of the company).

This theory is the reason why there is so much information about directors' dealings and why such a fuss is made if directors buy or sell their shares. If directors are seen buying shares in their companies, the market sees this as positive and assumes the directors know the company is doing well and the share price will rise. On the flip side, if directors sell their shares, it's perceived as them knowing something the rest of us don't.

Now you must remember that company directors are real people who live real lives. Maybe the company director needs to sell shares to pay for a new house, a wedding, or a divorce. There could be a whole stream of reasons why a director needs to sell shares. But if several senior directors all hold a significant number of shares, and they all sell them in one go, as investors we have a right to question why the company's management—who can see the future of that company and understand its prospects better than anybody—has decided to sell up and not participate financially in the future performance of the business.

Before you buy shares in a business, you should spend ten minutes learning about the managerial structure of the business and how management gets paid. We'll talk more about the annual report later, but in it you will see that a huge section is dedicated to directors' pay, what they earn, and how they get paid it (shares or cash). As a retail investor, it should give you more comfort to own a company where all the directors are also significant shareholders and get paid performance-related bonuses in shares. You should be even happier if they are buying more shares on top of those they already own.

Also keep an eye on the day-to-day news of a company, and make a note of which directors are selling and buying shares. If a loan director owns five hundred thousand shares and suddenly sells fifty thousand, don't panic. The director might just need the money to pay for children's school fees. However, if three or four company directors all start selling quantities of their shares, while talking positively about the future of the business, it might be time to worry.

One last thing about director's dealings. By law, they are only allowed to buy and sell shares at certain times of year. (It's usually a small window of time, just after company results or updates.) Don't be surprised when you see a cluster of director dealings all at the same time. It's because they are not allowed to buy and sell when they may want or need to. What's more important is whether the directors are buying or selling and the size of their transactions.

**Tip:** When company management buy shares in the company, this is positive, especially if several people are buying at the same time. The opposite is also true. If several managers sell at the same time, alarm bells should go off in your head.

## Changes to managerial teams

People come; people go. People get offered new jobs. People take retirement. People get sick and leave work. Just because somebody on the management team has resigned, that does not automatically constitute a crisis.

However, you need to keep an eye on this. If management is changing regularly, it could be a problem. If the finance director suddenly resigns, you should read the statements and try to understand why. If there is a whole host of changes at the top, something is probably wrong, and you should consider sitting back and watching how it develops.

If a company is doing well and loses a lot of its top management, it is probably negative. If a company is doing badly and loses a lot of its top management, it could be a positive sign and the start of a turnaround. The information on management changes is readily available for a retail investor and takes a couple of minutes to look up, so you really have no excuse.

## Institutional shareholders

By UK law, anybody who buys 3 percent of the voting rights of a listed UK company has to disclose this to the stock exchange, and this information will be released to everybody via newswires. That's why when you look at a company's news pages, you always see lots of news stories telling you that some professional pension fund you have never heard of has bought shares in the company.

Once somebody has purchased 3 percent of the voting rights, each and every time that person buys another 1 percent, this has to be disclosed to the marketplace. Once someone purchases 30 percent of the voting shares, UK law states that the person needs to launch a cash offer (takeover) for the remaining 70 percent of shares not owned already.

This means the information of anyone who owns more than 3 percent of shares in every listed company is available, and by law, anybody is allowed to see it. Only a handful of financial websites and brokers carry this information in an easy-to-consume table or list, and you need to find one.

This information is gold dust and well worth taking time to find. Imagine you are interested in buying a stock, Company X, and you look at the three leading shareholders, who each own around 10 percent. You write down their names and Google them. You then realize that the three biggest shareholders are long-term, value-seeking investors who invest on a five-to ten-year timeline. I'm not suggesting that we follow like sheep, but we have to have some trust that when three different professional companies have bought a significant amount of these shares, they believe it is an undervalued stock and it's a long-term investment. If you want to be super keen, you can even go back through all the old news stories and work out when these institutions bought the shares and what they paid for them. This would really back up your investment case.

However, Company Y has only one major shareholder, a hedge fund that owns 25 percent. You go to Google and read about the hedge fund. It turns out it is a shareholder activist, so it buys companies and tries to change them or break them up. If you buy shares in this company, you are in for a rocky ride, as at some point, the hedge fund will start a fight with the company management and try to get them removed or somehow change the business model. As an investor, you may or may not agree with the hedge fund, but you need to be aware of the fight that's about to happen.

For the last example, let's look at Company Z. The five largest shareholders are all pension funds that are focused on high dividend yields. Again, you are not a sheep, and you can think for yourself, but this tells you (far better than any bulletin board or taxi driver can) that this is stable company that professional investors feel will pay a good dividend for years to come.

I have to be honest. This is not always that easy. For example, you will see that some shares are owned by Legal & General, and when you go to their website, you realize that they have hundreds of different types of funds. You won't know if the "high-risk-and-growth fund" owns the shares or if the "safe-and-steady fund" owns them. When it does work, the information is priceless.

Again, the next time you switch brokers, maybe ask if it's a service they provide. It's worth paying a little extra for a broker if they are willing to provide up-to-date and reliable financial ratios and also offer support for things like institutional ownership and company management. FYI, market professionals will have a Bloomberg or Reuters terminal where they can find this information in a few clicks; it's literally a ten-second job for them. It's not a big deal for them to give you this type of information; it's just a question if they are willing to.

Knowing the type of large shareholders who own shares in a company is a lovely little bonus, as you can make sure your investment strategy matches theirs. If you are buying a share for the short term and rapid growth, and all the institutional investors are safe-and-steady-long-term players, you may have the wrong end of the stick, and it's worth restarting your research with an open mind. You never know; you may have spotted something they have not.

Always look out for a single shareholder who owns a significant amount of shares. That person can have a lot of control over the company, its management, and its future plans. If you buy shares in a company where a single shareholder owns 40 percent plus of the shares, you are really at that person's mercy.

## Short interest

This has nothing to do with attention spans and losing interest about something in a short time. Obviously, investors buy shares when they think the share price will go up, and they can short them (sell shares without owning them) when they think they are overvalued and will go down. It's worth doing a check to see what short interest is out there.

Again, all the information is out there for you. You just need to know where to look. Type the company you are interested in into Google, and then type "short interest."

Take the results with a pinch of salt, because there are a million ways a professional investor can hide being short a stock. However, this does give you a rough idea of what percentage of the market is shorting your stock because they think it's going down. If you are thinking of buying the stock, but the amount of short interest is high and getting higher, ask yourself why. Try to think about why they could see that the shares are overvalued and why they want to go short. Again, you could be right, and they could be wrong, but this information is out there and available, so use it.

## Key points from step 12

- Look to invest in companies where the management are also invested.

- Don't worry too much about the odd manager selling some of his or her shares, but do worry if managers are selling en masse.

- Watch out for a high turnover of staff in high managerial positions.

- Keep an eye on institutional ownership of shares. A single large shareholder can have a lot of influence over the business and its management.

- Watch out for significant changes in short interest.

As retail investors, we don't have the time, energy, resources, or even inclination to go into too much detail here, but if you can find a company that has growing earnings, low debt, good ROCE, and a long-term management team in place who understands the business, and those managers are invested in the business, it's another tick. In the perfect world, you are looking for a company that can run itself and whose earnings continue to increase regardless of its management.

There is another place to look for information, and that's analysts' forecasts and price targets, but that deserves a chapter on its own. Let's move on to step 13.

# Step 13:

# Analyst Price Targets, Forecasts, and Research Reports

Many retail investors use analyst reports and price targets to judge if a stock is good value or not. If you do this and only this, you are on dangerous ground.

### Don't trust investment-bank price targets

Let me explain a little background on investment banks. They are usually split into two teams and separated by an invisible wall called a Chinese wall. (A Chinese wall is used in businesses to try to stop information from flowing from one part of the business to another, thus preventing a conflict of interest.) One team deals with public stuff, and this is where their traders sit to try to make money and their stock analysts write research reports for distribution to the general public. On the private side of the investment bank, the bankers deal with advising companies and offering services that are confidential and that nobody should know about. If the private side gave the public side this information, the public would have "inside information" and could illegally make a lot of money by trading with knowledge that nobody else has.

The issue is that investment banks make a lot of money by offering services to companies, and this is a major revenue stream for them. It's really competitive, and lots of investment banks want this business. If the bankers on the private side of the investment bank advised a company that it should expand aggressively and buy a competitor, and then the analyst on the public side of the same investment bank released a report saying the M&A deal was terrible and would harm the company, that's obviously not a wonderful situation for either the company or the investment bank.

I'm not saying that the Chinese walls don't work. They do, and they are rigorously defended. Traders on the public side of investment banks do not get inside information. That's not what I am saying. However, if you look at which investment bank is advising the company (this information is nearly always available on the company's website; remember step 10) and then look at that investment bank's research report, coincidentally it's nearly always a buy rating with a price target significantly higher than where the shares are currently trading.

So you may be thinking, "Well, that's OK. Each company has two or three investment banks as advisers, so I can trust the other investment banks' research." I'm afraid you can't, because investment banks may want the listed company's business in the future, so they don't want to upset them now because it could hinder their relationship in the future. If you could just imagine a conversation like the following:

Investment banker: "Hello, M D of Company X. We are long-time admirers of your business and really want to work with you in the future. We think you have an amazing business, and we have loads of ideas about how you can increase profits and shareholder value."

M D of Company X: "Well, that's very nice, and I am pleased you like our company so much. So why has your investment bank rated us as a strong sell for the last five years and advised all your retail clients not to consider buying our shares?"

Can you see how that's an awkward conversation? Can you see why investment banks make sure they offer positive research reports?

You could now ask the question, what's the point of research analysts? Why have them at all? If you are a retail investor, you're absolutely right; they are of little value to us. However, for professional investors, they are still valuable indeed, as they are experts in their sectors.

If a stock is terrible but the relationship with the investment bank is important, some analysts will write a fair research report, pointing out all the issues and concerns, so the professional investor can "read between the lines." If you call and speak to research analysts over the phone or meet them face-to-face, they can often give a much fairer view about the company they are analysing. The problem is that as retail investors, we don't get to see the analysts' research reports, and we don't get to call them up for a chat, so this avenue is useless to us.

If you ever see an analyst report, I strongly recommend you read it. However, these reports are not available anywhere, and unless you are a client of a particular investment bank and pay a significant commission each year, you won't get to see them.

If, like a lot of retail investors, you currently use analysts' price targets a lot, and I am upsetting you at the moment, there is a possible way to use them if you want to do loads of work. Some investment banks write honest research with honest price targets. These tend to be about stocks in different countries where the investment bank does not have an office. It's unlikely a company will want banking advice from an investment bank that doesn't have any operations in that country. For example, a Spanish investment bank that does not have an office in the United Kingdom will probably write fair research about the stock.

> **Tip:** Understand the importance of analysts' forecasts. We have all seen (or will see) examples of a stock releasing negative earnings reports and the share price goes up, and a company releasing positive earnings but the share price goes down. That's because of the relationship between earnings and analysts' forecasts.
>
> For example, if all the research analysts report that earnings will rise by 25 percent, but then earnings only rise by 20 percent, the "market will be disappointed," and the shares will fall, despite the company posting a 20 percent rise in earnings.
>
> On the flip side, if analysts expect a £500 million loss for the year, but the company reports a £250 million loss, the share price will rise, as the "market has been surprised on the upside," even though the company is still making a loss.
>
> You need to understand the importance of analysts' forecasts versus actual results.

## Independent research

The main way you can trust analysts' price targets

and sell, hold, or buy recommendations is if the writer is independent. There are a number of small banks that don't have a corporate side (private side). There are also a number of small boutique research houses who write independent research reports. You can often buy their research for a small fee. The issue is (and I don't want to sound mean) that the best analysts work for the best investment banks, so you need to understand that the guys working at small banks or boutique research houses probably don't have the same knowledge or the same relationship with the company's management that the big banks do.

So there you go. Step 13 is to ignore all price targets and broker forecasts unless they are from small, independent banks or boutique research houses. Even so, take their recommendations with a pinch of salt. Don't assume that because they are "market professionals" you can trust everything they tell you.

## Key points from step 13

- Never trust an investment-bank price target if the bank is a company advisor or wants to be a company advisor (you will never know this).

- Normally the company website (corporate site) will have a list of contacts, and under those contacts will be a list of advisors. You will notice the advisors nearly always have a buy rating and a high price target.

- If you ever see a research report, read it. They are worth reading; just ignore the price target.

- In general, you can trust independent research, but it probably won't be the best quality.

- Understand the relationship between analyst forecasts and price movements.

Shall we get back to being positive again? Let's look at the next step, which is all about looking at the current stock price.

# Step 14:

# Technical Analysis and Picking a Potential Entry Level

Assuming the stock you have been researching has ticked every box so far, you will by now be thinking of pulling the trigger and buying some shares, but wait a little longer.

Just because you have found a good stock, that does not mean you should leap in and buy it right now. There are a number of things you need to think about. Slow this phase right down, and take some deep breaths. Each and every penny cheaper you buy the shares for makes a significant difference on your return. If you buy shares 2 or 3 percent cheaper than you were going to, that will make your return even better when you come to sell the shares in the future.

I hate to say it, but time and time again, history shows that retail investors as a group get easily caught up in the emotion of investing and let fear and greed dictate their actions. Don't let this be you.

Remember that you are trying to buy at a low price and sell at a high price. Don't be the retail investor who rushes in and pays any price at the wrong time. Make sure you pay the right price at the right time. Just spending time thinking and planning your po-tential entry level can save you a fortune and boost your investment returns.

### Separate finding a good share from buying it

It's going to sound like I am continuously stopping you from trading, but that's not the case. I'm trying to remove any emotion from your trading. As George Soros said, "If investing is entertaining, if you're having fun, you're probably not making any money. Good investing is boring."

When most people buy a house or a car, they haggle over the price. Before booking a holiday, some people wait months to see if the travel agent offers any discounts. Consumers buy in bulk from supermarkets when there is a special deal. All these sensible and sane people turn into completely different types of people when they become retail investors and buy shares. The same people who research a car in meticulous detail will plunge into the stock market and buy shares at any price, often on the back of a tip from a bulletin board or taxi driver.

Just because you have found a good share that meets all your investment criteria, that does not mean you have to buy it right away. Look at the share charts, and look at where it has traded in the last few months. Has it been lower at any point?

Understand whether the share is highly correlated with the index it's in. If the market has a 10 percent correction (goes lower), will your target shares also go down? Is the share price of the company you are interested in highly correlated to oil prices or commodities? If you are thinking of buying a mining stock that looks really undervalued, but commodity prices are going down, the mining company's price will probably get knocked down with them. I am not saying not to buy the undervalued mining company's shares. Put them on your watch list, and buy them when the time is right.

Look at how the shares react when there is no related news announced. For example, if the company has not announced any news or numbers, yet the share price is still moving around aggressively, there is something else driving the share price. This means that if you sit and wait, you may be able to get it at lower prices as the general market ebbs and flows.

Remember, your number-one goal when investing is to not lose money. Protect your money at all costs, and don't be the investor who pays the top price. Be the boring investor who doesn't let emotions get in the way. Be the boring investor who finds a stock he/she desperately wants to invest in but then waits six weeks and buys at a 6 percent lower price.

To put it another way, the top fund managers (professionals who invest other people's money) roughly outperform the market by 10 to 12 percent each year. As a retail investor, if you just think about execution and not rushing into stocks, you can probably save yourself 5 to 6 percent a year, so you are halfway there just by prolonging the period between finding a good stock and buying it.

## Consider technical traders

This is a huge subject, and I could easily write a book on this topic alone. Without going into too much detail, there are a huge number of people (retail investors and market professionals) who consider themselves to be technical traders, and we need to understand what they do and why they do it. You don't need to be an expert, but you need to have a rough understanding.

Technical traders disagree with everything I have written about in this book. They don't believe in P/E ratios, and they are not worried about company debt. Technical traders never bother opening the company report or looking at the balance sheet. They believe the market is already 100 percent efficient, and the most accurate way to see what the price of a company should be is to look at the current share price.

To put it another way, imagine a hypothetical world where you could freeze time. Right now in this frozen time, you gather all the people in the whole world who are interested in a particular stock—retail investors, professional investors, hedge funds, company management, accountants, auditors, investment-bank analysts, and so on—and put them in a single room. Imagine you could give them a detailed questionnaire and extract all the information about the company from them: their opinions, their emotions, and their predictions for the future. Now imagine if you could feed all that information into a hypothetical computer program to give you the exact share price the stock should be trading at, given every factor, emotion, and prediction from all the people in the room. A technical trader believes our hypothetical computer program would come up with exactly the same price as the current price in the stock market.

So technical traders see no value in fundamental research and are not worried about sales forecasts or regulatory changes that affect the company. They believe that all the information they need is already shown in the current share price.

So technical traders study graphs and stock charts and look for patterns that will predict the future. Remember, we can fill a book on this subject, so I can't explain each and every thing they are looking for. But, for example, if a share price trades between 150 and 200 for any length of time, technical traders will say the stock is trading in a channel. When the shares get to 150, they will buy them, with a stop-loss at 145, and when the shares get to 200, they will go short them, with a stop-loss of 205.

If the shares continue to rise to 210, technical traders call this a "breakout" and will buy the shares as the price moves up. Now, you may think this is crazy. They are happy to short a stock at 200, but a few minutes later, when it rises to 205 they want to buy it? Technical trading is a topic on its own and a unique science. You may not agree with technical traders or what they do, but to be a good retail investor, you need to acknowledge their existence and the potential impact they can have on share prices.

As a retail investor, you need to look at the stock chart of your company for the last six months or so and identify if there are any clear channels or not. If you can identify support lines and resistance lines, you should factor this into your trading. For example, if you are thinking of buying shares and you see that the current share price is right at the high end of a channel or, better still, at the resistance point, sit back and wait and see if the technical traders push it down lower for you.

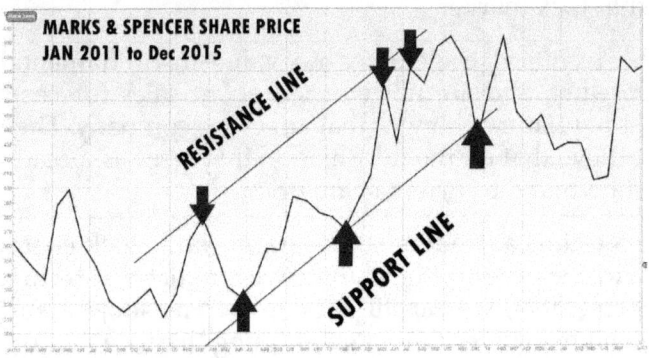

We'll talk in detail about stop-losses in the next chapter (step 15), but never put your stop-loss just above a resistance level. You may as well put your stop-loss on the other side of a resistance channel and see if the technical traders keep the price away from your stop for you.

As a retail investor, you won't have time to sit and study charts all day looking for head-and-shoulder patterns or calculating the McClellan Oscillator, and I am not going to go into them in this book. However, by looking at a chart, you should be quickly able to identify any support and resistance levels (if there are any), and just being aware of these levels can often save you 4 or 5 percent on the price you finally buy your shares at.

> **Tip:** Don't bother learning about technical trading in too much detail.
>
> People often come to my seminars and talk about "placing orders at the first bullish candlestick on the MACD cross-and-signal line," while looking for "round bottom" and "triple top" chart indicators. I have to be honest; I was a professional trader inside major investment banks for over ten years, and I still don't understand a lot of what technical traders talk about.
>
> Unless you are going to start trading full time (sitting at a desk for eight hours a day), don't worry about the details. Use a chart to identify a trend (going up or down) and to identify support and resistance lines, and that's all you need to know. Having the knowledge that technical traders are out there and can offer support and resistance is important.
>
> Why try to get hundreds of tiny share-price moves right when you just need to get one major decision right, and then you can sit back and relax?

## The trend is your friend; never fight the trend

While looking at the chart, try to identify if there is a clear trend. If the share price is in an obvious downtrend, do not buy. This is called trying to catch a falling knife, and just don't attempt to do it. I would rather watch a stock go down to its low, rebound, and rise by 10 percent again before I step in and buy. I would rather miss that first 10 percent so that I know it's no longer in a downtrend than try to catch that falling knife.

You also need to step back and look at the general market conditions. If you have already established that your stock is highly correlated with the FTSE, look at what level the FTSE is currently at. Look back at the last twenty years of the FTSE 100 Index, and you will see that it's clearly in a channel, trading between four thousand and sixty-five hundred points, with the occasional dip below four thousand points when the market was feeling doomed and above sixty-five hundred when it was feeling euphoric. If you are buying a share that's highly correlated to the FTSE when the FTSE is trading above sixty-five hundred points, you are in for a world of pain. Similarly, if you are thinking of buying a highly correlated stock when the FTSE is below four thousand points, I suggest you fill your boots and get involved.

As Warren Buffet put it, "Be fearful when others are greedy, and greedy when others are fearful."

## Beware of bull markets, and understand market psychology

Again, the subject of market psychology is a book all on its own.

I once read a quote by a professional fund manager. I think it may have been Peter Lynch, but I can't be sure, so I'm sorry if I have credited the wrong person. Basically it goes along the following lines:

I know we are at the bottom of a bear market when I am at a dinner party with people who don't work on Wall Street, and nobody will talk to me, and they would rather chat to a dentist. I know we are in a bull market when the same people at the same dinner party come up to me and ask me for share tips. I know when we are at the top of the bull market when the same people at the same dinner party come up to me and tell me what stocks and shares I should be buying for my fund.

I have probably decimated that quote and credited the wrong person, but I think it's really nice and gets my point across. Retail investors have a reputation for jumping into the market at the very top, when prices are at their most expensive.

I think retail investors have this reputation because a bull market can drag up all share prices — not just the good companies but also some of the mediocre ones. That means a bull market can make poor investors money as well as good ones. The poor investors tell their friends and family how easy it is to make money, and more retail investors join in, hoping for the same success. They tell their friends how easy it is, and so on. At the very top of a bull market is when most retail investors are buying shares for the first time, and, hey, presto, suddenly the bubble pops, and they lose loads of money.

Ironically, these same retail investors will hold the shares they bought at the very top of the market for longest, as they hope the share price will return to those dizzy heights. By the time the stock market hits rock bottom and the bear market is about to turn into a bull market again, many retail investors are so bruised and battered and have lost so much money that they have no interest in buying shares at rock-bottom prices. In fact, at this point, they have no interest in the stock market at all. They have no interest in the low prices of shares, or at least not until they are near the top of the next bull market, and their friends and family are telling them how easy it is to make money again.

If I have just described you, or you think I'm being smug, you should know that I was a beginner during the dotcom bubble. The first shares I ever owned were during the dotcom bubble, and I joined the ranks of excited retail investors who paid silly prices for tech stocks at the top of the market. When the bubble burst, I did not have stop-losses in place, and I held a really dodgy portfolio of massively over-valued random tech shares in the hope they would go back up. To make matters worse, I even bought more of some of those shares to "average down" my entry price. Rage Software was a maker of computer games for PlayStation, and I actually tried to catch the falling knife four or five times before it finally went bust and put me out of my misery.

I still hold some of those dodgy tech shares today, and those that have not gone bust are still worthless or are trading at only a few pence. I actually have one of the share certificates on my wall to remind me to never to be such a fool ever again.

Do not be one of those retail investors who pay the top price for shares. Never join in at the top of the bull market. If you can't help yourself, or you didn't spot the top of the bull market and suddenly realize you are on the other side (that's OK; it happens—nobody sounds an alarm to tell you it's the top), just make sure you cut your losers so you can fight another day and have cash available to pick up some bargains after the market has adjusted.

### If it's a small (illiquid) stock, don't buy in the first hour

If you are buying a major FTSE or DOW stock, don't worry about this at all. But if you are buying a smaller company (with a market cap under £250 million), you may find that it's illiquid (meaning not many people buy or sell shares in it each day).

If you are buying an illiquid stock, never buy early in the morning. It often takes a while for professional investors to come in and narrow the spread. For your information, every share has a spread. That's the difference between the highest price a buyer is willing to buy at and the lowest price a seller is willing to sell for. Early in the morning, buyers and sellers have often not put their orders in, and the spreads are really wide. If you buy shares at this time, you may be paying a higher price than if you waited until midmorning. I just want to articulate this again. If you buy shares 3 or 4 percent cheaper just by following these boring and dull rules, that's a 3 or 4 percent better return on your investment already. You can get a better rate of return than you can in a bank account just by getting the best execution possible.

## Key points from step 14

- Remember, a company's share price can move around aggressively in the short term; this is despite there being little change to the underlying value of the business (remember Mr. Market and his mood swings).

- Finding a good company in which to invest is completely different from finding the right time to invest in it.

- Be patient and wait for the right time to buy the shares. If you miss the opportunity and the shares go higher, so what? You have lost nothing! There will be another great stock just around the corner.

- If it's a small, illiquid stock, don't buy or sell in the first hour or two.

- Spend time and effort looking at the charts, picking resistance and support levels, and understanding what phase the market is in before you buy.

- In general, spend more time researching the shares you are about to buy than you would for a new car or holiday or washing machine.

- Never join the stampede who join in the fun and games at the top of the bull market when it looks so easy to make money.

- When the markets are at their lowest ebb and most depressed, that's the time to buy shares, and buy lots of them.

- This is very crude, but look at it this way. In general, the closer the FTSE 100 Index gets to trading at four thousand points, you should be buying good shares with good prospects with a long-term view. If the FTSE 100 Index is trading above sixty-five hundred, you should be looking to take profits, not joining in and buying at the top of the market to make easy, quick money.

Now that we've done research on the share price, how it moves, and what condition the general market is in, we can move on to the next chapter. Step 15 is the final step. This could be the final stage before we go ahead and pull the trigger and become part owners of a real company that employs real people and sells real products and services.

# Step 15:

# Risk-versus-Reward Analysis and Stop-Loss Levels

So this is it, the final step before you call your broker or log into your trading account and click the "buy" button that always looks so tempting. There are a few last things we need to do, however. We need to make 100 percent sure that we are doing the right thing for the right reason.

We need to make sure we have an open mind, a plan, and an idea of risk versus reward; and most importantly, we need a correct level for our stop-loss. Putting a stop-loss in place is crucial. You may be thinking that if you have completed steps 1 to 15, you are onto a surefire, guaranteed winner, but there is no such thing. Even after following these steps, around 40 percent of the shares you invest in will be the wrong calls. For one reason or another they will go down. That's absolutely fine, and we can live with only being right 60 percent of the time, just as long as we have a stop-loss level in place so we can get rid of our losers, and we are disciplined and let our winners win.

> Tip: You don't get a nice garden by cutting down the flowers in bloom and spending loads of time treating and watering the weeds. Cut your losers, and let your winners win.

On that note, let's crack on and have a look at some key things you need to think about before pressing that lovely, enticing, and tempting buy button.

### Confirmation bias

This is an investor's enemy, and you need to fight

against seeking out what the clever psychologists call confirmation bias. It's basically in human nature to make a decision and then look for as much evidence as you can to back you up and enforce that you made the correct decision.

For example, take Sam, our friend from Sheffield who likes curry and Coronation Street. Sam also likes a girl in his workplace named Sarah, and Sarah likes him, but neither of them have the confidence to ask the other out. Again, that's not really relevant, but I thought it was interesting.

Sam decided to buy a car a few years back, and he started the process with an open mind. Sam had no idea if he wanted a Ford, Volkswagen, or Nissan, so he did lots of research. After reading loads of websites, reviews, and car magazines and watching car TV shows, he decided he wanted to buy a VW Golf. After he made his decision, it took him another three months to take the plunge and go to the VW garage and pay his money.

However, when he finally did and got his car home, Sam was really happy. But there was a nagging doubt that he had done the right thing and bought the right kind of car. Sam started looking at VW message boards on the Internet, and they made him happy, because hundreds of people were writing messages about how great VW Golfs are. He got an old car magazine out and reread the article about how good the VW Golf car is. He went to the pub and had a long chat with a friend who also had a VW Golf, knowing his friend often talked about how good his car was. Sam was doing what we all do. It's in our nature. Once you have made a decision, you look for confirmation bias to back it up and make you feel 100 percent sure you made the right decision.

As a retail investor, confirmation bias is your enemy. You need to guard against it at all times. If you look for positive reinforcement of your investment, you will find like-minded people who will be happy to give it to you. Don't go looking! Value your own opinion far more than the opinion of a complete stranger who knows less about investing than you do.

Actually, as a retail investor, you need to do the opposite. You should always be looking for evidence that you made a mistake, and you should question yourself at all times. If the share price rises and you start making money, don't assume it's because you are an investing genius. Instead, try to understand what is causing the move. Is it earnings, is it news about a new product or client, are the directors buying their own shares, or is it just because the whole market has gone up and your stock has been dragged higher along with it? Do the same if the shares move against you. Is it the general market, or is there a stock-specific reason for the decline? This self-analysis is a lot more valuable than going to a message board and asking other retail investors for confirmation bias.

## SWOT analysis

So what's SWOT analysis? This sounds technical and difficult, and it must involve lots of mathematics. This is a really simple technique used in business to analyse the strengths, weaknesses, opportunities, and threats of a business, a business plan, or even a specific decision within the business. It's seldom used in the investment world, but I use it all the time, and it really helps clarify my thinking.

Take a piece of paper, and draw a horizontal line across the middle of the page and a vertical line down the centre so that you have four equally sized boxes. At the top of each box, write either "Strengths" or

"Weaknesses" or "Opportunities" or "Threats." (It's really that easy.) Hey, presto, you now have what's called a "SWOT matrix," which I personally think sounds like a Hollywood action movie starring Tom Cruise.

Now comes the difficult part. You need to take just about every relevant piece of information you know and place it in one of the above boxes. For example, a company you are looking at might have a good P/E level, and you would consider that a strength, so write it in the Strengths box. The company may have poor debt, and you consider that a weakness, so write it in the Weaknesses box. The company may be a possible takeover target, which you think is an opportunity, so write that in the Opportunities box. Finally, the company might be faced with a new, aggressive competitor, which you think is a risk, so (you guessed it) write that in the Threats box.

In theory, the Strengths and Weaknesses boxes should be full of the information that is relevant now (so things we know as facts, like ratios and company management). Again, in theory, the Opportunities and Threats boxes are more generalized, looking at factors outside of the company and things that may or may not happen.

Every relevant piece of information you have should have a place in one of the four boxes. I would expect to see information about market caps, current and historic share prices, all your ratios (EPS, PEG, EV/EBITDA, book value, debt ratio, etc.), dividend payments, company management, product information, competitors' information, positive and negative news stories, any relevant information from the company's website or annual report, and so on. Put everything relevant into the SWOT analysis.

Take your time and do this exercise thoroughly, because SWOT analysis is only as good as the information you put in. You also need to be honest with yourself. You can make the worst news possible seem like an "opportunity" if you want to manipulate the process.

Once you have finished your SWOT analysis, your piece of paper should help you clarify your thinking about the investment. If there are loads of items in the Strengths and Opportunities boxes, you could be onto a winner. However, if your Weaknesses and Threats boxes are well populated, maybe pass on this one.

Using SWOT is a simple, quick, and easy way to visually see all the different factors we have looked at. If you have gone through steps 1 to 14, you will have several sheets of paper with all sorts of different facts and comments written down about the company, its sector, its competitors, and the general market. SWOT is the one tool you have to see all these different things in a matrix, so take the time and do a proper and honest SWOT for each and every investment. You will be amazed at how this simple process makes complicated investments look straightforward.

## Risk-versus-reward analysis

Investing money in the stock market has a high degree of risk, and if you're going to take the risk, the amount of money you stand to gain needs to be big—far bigger than the amount of money you stand to lose.

Let's chat about Sam again, our football-loving, Sunday-roast-dinner-eating friend from Sheffield. He does all his shopping online, for your information, apart from bread, which he likes to squeeze before he buys a loaf. Again, that's not relevant, but I thought it was interesting.

Sam did a load of research on a share, and he is about to buy five hundred shares of Company X. The price of Company X was 300p a few weeks ago (an all-time high), but four months ago, the shares were trading at 200p. The current share price of Company X is 280p. Sam thinks it's bound to go back up to the all-time high of 300p soon, and he will make 20p profit. However, he sees the maximum downside as 200p, which it could go back to if it continues to fall. Sam's risk-versus-reward profile on this trade is not great. He has a 20p upside and an 80p downside. That's a terrible risk/reward profile; he should look to invest in something with an 80p upside and a 20p downside.

There is a very simple ratio you can use to calculate risk-versus-reward profiles. Take the amount of money you stand to make from the trade, and divide it by the total money invested in the trade, and that will give you your risk-versus-reward calculation.

For Sam's investment in Company X above,

$$\frac{\text{20p profit on 500 shares} = £100 \text{ profit}}{\text{500 shares} \times \text{280p} = £1400 \text{ total investment}} = 0.07 \text{ Risk/reward calculation}$$

No professional investor would invest with a risk/reward profile of 0.25 or less, let alone 0.07. Remember Sam could probably get a risk free 5% return by putting his money in a long-term savings account. Why is he taking the risk of losing money for such a pitiful return?

So calculate your risk-versus-reward profile, and don't invest in anything where the odds are not in your favour. You can see the need for honesty, because you can easily distort your upside and downside to give you a more favourable ratio, but why would you? You'd only be tricking yourself.

## Trading plan

An investor without a clear plan and investment objectives is like a baby trying to force a triangle-shaped block through a circle-shaped hole. The baby will occasionally get lucky and find the triangle-shaped hole, but it's a long, frustrating process that relies more on luck than on skill or analysis.

Before you invest, you need to write a trading plan. This does not have to be a five-hundred-page risk assessment. It can simply be one side of a sheet of A4 paper, but you need a plan. You need to write down the reasons you are buying the share. You need to write down the price you want to buy the shares at, and you need to write down anything that can affect the share price in the future (dates of earnings, dividend payments, etc.).

You need to calculate at what price you will admit you have got it wrong and close out the position, and you also need to calculate a realistic price at which you would sell the shares. If you are still happy to invest, you need to keep this trading plan on hand and refer back to it on a regular basis.

> **Tip:** Always remember, in 2016 you could earn a risk-free 3 percent or maybe even up to 5 percent return by leaving your hard-earned money in a high-interest savings account or investing in a risk-free government bond. Can I repeat, that's a *risk-free* return!
>
> If you are going to invest in stocks and shares, you need to be taking the risk for significantly more than a 4 percent or 5 percent return. If you are going to risk your own money, I always think the return should be at least dou-

ble what you would get in a bank. This figure goes higher as the risk of the investment goes higher.

Always view the investment you are about to make, and the possible return you will get, against leaving your money in a high-interest savings account. I would take a risk-free 5 percent return over a risky possible 7 percent return any day of the week!

## The "margin of safety" calculation

You may remember in step 2 we spoke about Benjamin Graham, who came up with the fictional Mr. Market to describe the wild fluctuations in share prices. Graham was a value investor, meaning he would only buy shares in companies that he thought were significantly undervalued and then wait until the market corrected itself and valued them at the right price. He was very successful with this long-term strategy, as have been many value investors who followed in his footsteps (e.g., Warren Buffett).

The other major thing Graham is famous for is the "margin of safety" calculation.

Graham advocated looking at a company in some significant detail and calculating a fundamental (intrinsic) value for that company. Then he would only buy shares in that company if the share price was below the fundamental value together with a margin of safety, just in case he had got any calculations wrong, incorrectly predicted any future earnings, or been overoptimistic about the outlook of the company.

So, for example, if Graham valued a business at 200p, he may add on a 25 percent margin of safety and so would only buy the shares if and when they were for sale at 150p or lower. Graham argued that the larger the margin of safety, the bigger the buying opportunity was.

This is an incredibly simple concept, and one we all use in our everyday lives. For example, you may be driving on a motorway where the speed limit is seventy miles per hour, but if there is a lot of traffic and thick fog, you may decide to adopt a margin of safety and only drive at fifty miles per hour.

As retail investors, it's really hard for us to calculate a reliable fundamental value of a company on our own, and we need to rely on other data sources and other people's forecasts for our information; so the bigger margin of safety you can build in, the better.

## Stop-loss limits

I have saved the best for last. The very final thing you need to think about is where your stop-loss limit is positioned. This takes a considerable amount of skill and judgement.

A lot of retail investors use the 10 percent rule, which basically means that if shares go down 10 percent, you will automatically be stopped out. This rule is better than no rule, but in my opinion, it's far too simplistic.

You need to give your shares a chance to succeed, so you need to give your shares room to express themselves. There is nothing worse than doing a load of research and buying the right shares, but due to a little general market volatility at the start of your investment, you get stopped out and lose 10 percent, when the shares go up 50 percent over the long run.

At the same time, you need to be decisive and protect yourself from losing money at all times, so calculating the right stop-loss level is a skill within itself.

The way I do it is to try to separate general market noise and share-price moves from the fundamental things that drive a share price. For example, if I buy shares in a company and there is no news at all from the company, but the share price drops 10 percent alongside all the major indices like FTSE, CAC, DAX, DOW, and so forth, then I won't panic, and I will go with the flow (as long as the general markets are at a sensible level).

However, if I buy shares and the share price drops on the back of a negative news story or a negative set of earnings, or company directors start selling their shares, I will sell as soon as possible and will cut my position without any hesitation.

To conclude, you want to try to give your investments room to succeed, while being ruthless and disciplined in cutting your losing positions. I would be happy to buy shares and immediately put a 10 percent stop-loss limit on them, but I would keep an eye on the share price. If it started to fall, but there was no fundamental change to the company or any of the reasons why I originally invested, I would be inclined to give it some more room.

One last thought about stop-losses is that they are never guaranteed. More often than not, major news announcements happen once markets are closed or in the morning before markets open. For example, if a company is announcing a profit warning or takeover, they may do it at six thirty or seven in the morning to give the market time to digest the news before shares open at eight for trading. Shares often open at the new price rather than opening at yesterday's price and falling.

For example, let's say you buy shares at 200p with a stop-loss limit of 190p. That night, shares close at 205p, but before the market opens the following day, the company comes out with a major profit warning, and the shares open at 170p. The shares never traded at 190p or 180p, so your stop-loss can't be executed at those levels. Your stop-loss will be executed at the first available price, which will be 170p. So you see, a stop-loss never gives you 100 percent protection.

## Will you be able to sleep at night?

If you buy these shares, will you be able to sleep at night? If the answer is no, step back and think again. If from the moment you press the buy button, your stomach gets butterflies and you feel you have done the wrong thing, sell them again straight away.

If you are investing with money you can't afford to lose or you have nagging doubts about the investment you have just made or are about to make, don't do it. Success with investing is about having no emotions and being disciplined, and you are already off on the wrong course. Stop, and start looking for a new company to buy.

## Final thoughts on step 15

You must have a plan. You must have a stop-loss level, and you must have clearly defined reasons as to why you are buying the shares and what the triggers will be that move the share price higher. If you don't, you are setting yourself up for failure.

You need to understand that some things you will invest in will go down and will lose you money. This is a fact of life. Not a single professional investor in the world has a 100 percent success level. Investing is all about admitting when you got it wrong and losing as little money as possible. Investing is also about having targets in mind for your winners and not trading out of your winners too soon.

I have one last trick that I want to pass on to you, as

it's helped me a lot throughout the years. Despite all the research and ratios we do, I (and we all need to) still rely on my gut instinct a lot. Sometimes an investment feels right, and sometimes it feels wrong, and sometimes there is so much noise in the way that you no longer know if it's right or wrong. Life for a retail investor is hard. Family, hobbies, holidays, and work all get in the way, and sometimes it's difficult to know your own feelings about the stocks and shares you own when there is so much else going on in your life. When my mind is frazzled and I don't know if I should be in a trade or not, I sometimes trade out of the position and sleep on it.

It's amazing how effective I find this technique. If you go home without a position you think you should have, you will get one of two feelings. You may be relieved that you no longer have the position and no longer have to worry about it, in which case you have done the right thing by trading out. The alternative is you feel strongly that you made a mistake and can't believe you no longer have the exposure to the upside, which deep down you know is coming. If that's the case, buy the shares back the following morning.

This is an expensive process when you add on brokerage fees, stamp duty, and any possible price moves you may miss, but it's amazing how not having a position for twenty-four hours can clarify your thinking and get you back in line with your gut instinct. I don't do this all the time, but it really helps me clarify my thinking when I'm at the stage of an investment when I don't know if I should buy more, sell, or hold my shares.

Key points from step 15

- Fight against confirmation bias at all times.
- Draw up a quick and simple SWOT analysis.

Be honest with yourself; the only person you will be cheating is you!

- Conduct risk-versus-reward analysis, and only invest if it's in your favour.

- Have a trading plan and check back on it regularly.

- The bigger the margin of safety, the better.

- You will get things wrong, or the company could change; this happens. Set a stop-loss level that cuts positions you get wrong but also gives the company room to breathe and express itself.

- Make sure you can sleep at night.

- If you get yourself in a mess and have a cluttered mind, trade out. Having no position will clarify your thinking. If you instinctively feel you have done the wrong thing, trade back in with a clear and uncluttered mind.

So that's it, the end of step 15. There is just one last thing I want to chat about, and that's making money when markets are falling by going short. It does not really fit in anywhere else, so I have a short section next where I want to cover it.

# Conclusion to Phase 2

That's it! Congrats! You made it to the end of phase 2. You now have a really good understanding of what you need to look at when deciding if you want to invest or not.

Let's just assume you have found a winner and have identified a company you want to invest in. You are happy with the financials, profits are rising, debt is under control, the company is using its assets effectively, the company management is strong and stable, and its annual report reads well. You have made the decision that you want to invest!

What you do next is crucial; timing is everything. You have done so much work to get to this stage, you will be convinced the stock price is moon bound. You will be afraid you are going to miss the opportunity and may be willing to pay whatever it takes to get invested.

This is where patience and discipline are your best friends. Make sure you follow your investing plan and stick to your entry points. People buy good companies at the wrong price all the time. Just because you have found a good company, that does not mean you have found a good investment. Being a good investor is about finding good companies and investing at the right time. This may mean you miss this opportunity; so be it! It's better to have a smaller portfolio of investments you got at the right price that snap up every opportunity at any price.

Be patient; if you can buy your target company next month 5 percent cheaper, that's ultimately going to make your returns better by 5 percent! If you were shopping for groceries in Tesco, you would spend a few seconds analysing prices and making sure you get the best deal possible. Do the same for your investments. Every penny you save when buying stocks stays in your pocket; don't just give that money away to your counterpart in the marketplace.

You may have identified a beauty of a company. It may tick all the above boxes. But if that company's share price is highly correlated with the price of the FTSE 100 index and the index is at an all-time high, you need to ask if it's the right time to invest. Also if it's a good company but the share price is low because the index is low and falling, you need to be brave! Have conviction; the market prices things too high in bull markets and too low in bear markets. If you can buy good companies at low prices during bear markets, you will do extremely well over the long term. You have to be brave at these times. At the top of a bull market, everybody will be positive and telling you valuations are cheap and the outlook of the economy is great. At the bottom of a bear market, everybody will be scared and negative and telling you valuations are expensive and the outlook of the economy is terrible. It's at these moments as retail investors we need to excel!

You also need to accept you may have got your investment wrong! I hate to tell you this, but the company website and company annual report will describe the business as positively as possible. They may be lying to you, and you have absolutely no way of realizing it. Factors beyond your control may change the outlook of the business; you have absolutely no way of controlling them. Competitors can develop a better product, trends can change, sectors can fall out of fashion. You cannot control any of these things, so just take it on the chin and move on.

If you invest in your chosen company but the story changes, cut it. Get rid of it! Don't lose any sleep over it! If the business has hidden a major fall in sales by using creative accounting, that's their issue not yours. If you have made a mistake, or the story has changed, take the loss and move on. Do not wait or hope things are going to get better. Cut your losers loose!

Remember the golden rule. All you need to do is get more right than wrong, let your winners win, and cut your losers, and you will be fine! I know it's basic, but you will be amazed how few retail investors act this way! If you are currently sitting on a load of rubbish stocks, hoping for a miracle that they will get back to the price you paid for them so you don't have to realize the loss, you need to look in the mirror. Unless you can, with your hand on heart, say that the pattern of behaviour will change, maybe you should not make any more investments until you sort this psychological issue out.

You also need to adjust to making money. Once you pick a winning investment, don't be in a rush to sell it. Let it run, and see where it will take you. Before you sell a winning investment, do all the above research again from scratch and ask yourself, "Would I buy this company again today at these prices?" If the answer is yes, don't sell it. If you are not sure, consider selling half your position, and leave the other half invested. Again, you need to be truthful with yourself! If you have a history of selling successful investments too soon, you need to ask yourself why. This is another important pattern of behaviour that needs to change.

If you can follow the fifteen-step process outlined in this book to identify decent companies and wait to invest until the time is right, if you can admit you were wrong and cut losing positions, and if you can sit tolerantly watching your investments going up without the desire to sell them early, you will be a very successful retail investor!

# A Quick Note on Short Selling

Just when you thought it was all over, I go and pull a major subject out like this. I do, however, want to cover this subject. Some professional investors (mostly long-only pension-fund managers) are morally outraged about going short and don't think it's fair.

Well, I don't care! For the record, I don't think it's fair that professional investors have Bloomberg and Reuters terminals and access to advanced trading systems, research analysts, and company management. That's not fair, so I am happy to level the playing field each and every chance I get.

I am personally really comfortable "going short." The reason for this is because I became a market professional just after the dotcom boom and bust. For the first two years of my trading job at HSBC, stocks just went down. I was actually shocked when they started going up. I think it's because of this "accident of timing" that I am personally more worried about buying shares when markets are high than buying them when valuations are low.

I have spoken a lot about market direction and buying shares when the market is low and depressed. However, just for the record, at this point, I am talking about larger stocks that are highly correlated to the index they are in. I am not talking about small-cap stocks that can continue to go up because they are a good company, even when the general market is going down.

During my investing lifetime, I have made good returns by shorting stocks and the general market indexes at times when Mr. Market is being silly and offering ridiculously high prices. I have no moral remorse at all from doing this, and I strongly suggest you don't either.

Please note, investing and "outperforming the market" is different from making money. If the market is down 20 percent and you are only down 15 percent, well done; you have outperformed the market by 5 percent, but you have still lost 15 percent. We want to make money when stocks are falling as well as rising. If we are not comfortable doing this (if you are morally outraged), you should at least sell your stocks when the market is high, wait for the market to fall, and buy them back again at lower prices.

Again, I am just talking about the larger stocks that are highly correlated to the leading market indexes.

## What is "going short"?

This basically means selling shares you don't own and betting that the share price is going to go down rather than up.

It works in exactly the same way as buying shares, just in reverse.

## Understand the risks!

The main difference between buying shares and selling shares is that your losses are unlimited, and this scares a lot of people.

For example, if you buy one thousand shares of Company A at £1 a share, you have invested £1000. If the company goes bust, you could lose all your money, but you know you will only lose £1000. So your loss is locked at £1000 in the worst-case scenario.

However, if you go short one thousand shares of Company A at £1 a share, in theory your losses are unlimited. If you have got it wrong and the shares go up to £2 per share, you have lost £1000, but what if it continues to go up to £3, £4, or even £700 per share? You could end up owing £700,000. Some people really can't cope with this risk, and I totally get and understand that! I would never recommend that you invest in something you are not comfortable with. However, if you can get comfortable and manage your risk using stop-loss levels and so on, you can make money.

## SUK and SUK2 shares

Have a look at SUK and SUK2 shares. These are listed shares you would buy and sell in exactly the same way as Debenhams or Marks & Spencer.

The difference is that they track the FTSE 100 Index in reverse. So, for example, if you buy shares in SUK, they will go up if the FTSE 100 Index goes down, and down if the FTSE 100 Index goes up. So to be clear — if the FTSE 100 falls 5 percent, the shares you own will go up 5 percent.

SUK2 is exactly the same, but doubles the rate it tracks at. So, for example, if the FTSE 100 Index goes down 5 percent, your shares will go up 10 percent.

These are great for the retail investor and allow you to participate when the general markets are falling. The downside is, if you buy them at the correct time (when the FTSE is above seven thousand five hundred, for example), they are at their most expensive, and you won't be able to buy many shares without a significant amount of cash.

## Spread betting

I touched on this subject earlier in the book. Spread betting is relevant for retail investors. Again, you really need to get your head around the risks and understand how quickly you can lose money if you don't have stop-losses in place.

However, once you know how to spread bet, you can benefit from falling markets.

## Final thoughts about short selling

Going short is not for everybody, but unless you have a strong moral compass, you should consider it when Mr. Market is in his extreme mood and prices are too high.

If you also struggle with cutting losing positions, it's amazing how liberating it can be to make money from going short a stock. When you recondition your mind to making money by stocks going down, it's really difficult to sit with a long position you bought at the wrong time at the wrong price, which is losing a steady 5 percent a week, and not do anything about it.

# Conclusion

First things first. Congratulations for getting through my fifteen steps. I sincerely hope you have enjoyed reading this book, and I honestly hope you have found it useful.

Believe it or not, just by reading this book, you have propelled yourself into the top 5 percent of retail investors in this country. Most retail investors do not read books about investing or don't study anything new. Many continue to make the same mistakes and still practice the hope-to-get-rich-quick approach by borrowing other people's share tips and investing heavily in companies they know nothing about. You are different from them, and good for you.

I believe that the only way to succeed as a retail investor is to look for long-term value in shares and buy them at the right time.

I hate to tell you this in the last few pages, but you will never find the perfect stock. You will never find a stock that you can apply steps 1 to 15 to and get the perfect outcome with all the levels you want (if somehow you do, please drop me an e-mail telling me the name of the company). In this day and age, with so much information about stocks and shares bandied about the Internet and via financial-data providers like Bloomberg and Reuters and CNBC TV, you won't find an undervalued gem of a company that nobody else has noticed. In the 1930s this was possible, but in 2016 it's not. This is why I have put a modern spin on the traditional value-investing strategy.

Finding decent or good stocks is still possible, but to succeed you have to buy them at the right time. Timing is everything. If you follow all fifteen steps in detail and buy good-quality, undervalued stocks at the top of the bull market, you will lose a lot of money if the stocks are highly correlated to the index they're in. However, if you follow all fifteen steps and buy undervalued shares near the bottom of the next bear market, you will make a lot of money.

This is an extreme simplification, but think of it this way. In a bull market, all large cap shares go up. Good shares go up a lot, and bad shares go up a bit, but they all go up. In a bear market, all large-cap shares go down. Bad shares go down a lot, good shares go down a bit, but they all go down. Just remember this concept when you are next thinking about timing and when to buy or sell your investments. Small-cap stocks can fly against this concept, but for the large-cap stocks, it's rare that one goes consistently upwards while the market goes consistently downwards. If you spot one, it could be a great investment so research it!

Once you have mastered this book and its contents, the next thing you need to master is the ebbs and flows of the market, why it moves up and down, and what drives market sentiment. Once you can step back and watch the top of bull markets without greed, you are halfway there. When you can step in at the bottom of bear markets without fear, you are almost the complete package.

It's not just about the fifteen steps in this book. It's about understanding trends, market sentiment, and self-discipline. Time and again, history shows that retail investors get caught up in the emotion of investing and let greed and fear rather than knowledge and self-discipline dictate their actions. You, however, have to take a different approach.

The most important things you have to control as a retail investor are your discipline and emotions. Once you completely remove emotions from your investing and you have total and unwavering self-discipline, you have all the tools you need to succeed. When you should cut shares, you have to cut them. When you should leave shares to gain more, you have to leave them. This single skill is the most important talent you can give to yourself.

That's not to say you have to follow this book to the letter. There is plenty of room for you to grow and develop your own fifteen-step plan. You may decide that my whole chapter on debt was a waste of time, and you prefer to use the current ratio. That's absolutely fine and up to you; however, I will always argue that you need a mixture of quantitative and qualitative data to make good investment decisions.

Please remember that the skills you are learning in this book will be relevant for the rest of your life. I know phase 1 (the quantitative phase) was boring and dull. But once you know those ratios and how to apply them, you will have that knowledge forever. Fundamental investing is not a passing fad. It's not going out of fashion when some hotshot thinks of a new way to invest. Fundamental investing has been around for a long time, and it's always going to be around. For this reason, if any of the steps did not make sense, please go back and have another go. Once you master them, you will never have to relearn them.

If you enjoyed my book and you think it's helped you become a better investor, that's what I hoped for. We have plenty of other resources that can also help you at www.retail-investor-academy.com. Please feel free to visit the site and drop us a line and say hello and let us know how you are getting on. This book is a great first step, but if you want to go deeper and become a more advanced investor, we are here to help you.

Thanks again for reading this far, and I wish you every success and much happiness in your investing and in your life.

# Glossary

### Amortisation

Used by accountants, shows a routine (annual) decrease in value of an intangible asset over its life. For example, a company might put a monetary value on having a 10 year patent on a new product they have developed. Each year that passes, the value of that patent becomes less and less.

### Balance Sheet

Published each year by a company as part of its annual results, a balance sheet is a statement of the assets, liabilities, and capital of the business at a specific point of time.

### Bloomberg

The daddy of all financial platforms. Professional investors use Bloomberg terminals which gives them amazing data, news, charts and live company information. A Bloomberg terminal is expensive (think £25k a year) so outside the reach of most retail investors. Bloomberg also has a financial website and TV channel which can accessed by anybody. See also CNBC & Reuters.

### CNBC

A TV channel dedicated to the financial markets. Broadcasting live whenever and whereever the stock market is open. Well worth watching in the mornings between 7am and 8am if you have time. See also Bloomberg & Reuters.

## Depreciation

Used by accountants, shows a routine decrease in value of a tangible asset over its life. For example, an airline company might spend £50m buying a new plane it expects to last for 20 years, so they would depreciate the plane at £2.5m a year until it's worth nothing in year 20.

## Dividends

When a company makes a profit, it can decide to give some of that profit to shareholders in the form of dividends. Some companies pay regular dividends, some don't.

## Free Cash Flow

The amount of real cash a company has access to (left over) after it has paid all of its costs and maintained its assets. You want to invest in companies that can convert their profits into real, tangible cash. Free cash flow shows this.

## Fund Managers

A professional who is employed by a financial institution and manages investments on behalf of the company. Your pension will be in a fund, and this fund will be managed by a fund manager. They make decisions on what to buy and sell, and when.

## Income Statement

Sometimes called a profit & loss account, reports a company's financial performance over a certain period. It will typically list a company's major revenues and costs over the previous 12 months.

## Index

Each stock will be placed in an index. For example, the biggest 100 companies in the UK will be placed in the FTSE 100, the next biggest 250 will be placed in the FTSE 250. It's important to understand which index your stock is in, and how correlated your stock is to the performance of that index.

## Intangible asset

Assets that belong to a company that you can't physically touch. Things like patents, trademarks, copyrights, goodwill and brand recognition are all company assets, but you can't physically touch and feel them

## Liquidity

How many shares a company trades in a day. For example, a FTSE 100 company may trade millions of shares each day, so would be considered liquid. However a very small company may only trade a few hundred shares a day, and so would be considered illiquid. See also Volume and Market Maker.

## Market capitalization

Tells us how big a company is and what the market value of that company is. Take all the shares in issue and multiply against the current share price.

## Market Maker

A professional investor that works for a bank who agrees that they will always provide a bid and offer price for an illiquid stock. Market makers guarantee market liquidity for even the smallest of companies. See also Volume and Liquidity.

## Pension deficit

The amount of money a company owes to its workers' pension funds. A huge problem for some UK companies, which owe over half their value to their staff pension funds.

## Profit & Loss Account

Sometimes called an income statement, reports a company's financial performance over a certain period. It will typically list a company's major revenues and costs over the previous 12 months.

## Retail Investor

A retail investor is any non-professional investor. So anybody who invests in the stock market that does not work for a financial institution is considered a retail investor.

## Reuters

Another expensive news, data and live prices terminal used by professional investors. A Reuters terminal is cheaper than a Bloomberg terminal, but still out of reach of most retail investors. See also Bloomberg and CNBC.

## Sale and leaseback

The process whereby a company sells some of its assets and then leases them back. It provides a short-term cash injection, but results in less profits in the long term. Can be one of the first warning signs that all is not right with the business.

## Sector

Each stock is put in a market sector. This means that for example, all the retail stocks are grouped together in the retail sector, and all the banks are grouped together in the banking sector.

### Stake building

If a person or institution owns a large number of shares in a company, they are described as holding a stake in that company. You need to watch out for people increasing their stake in a company, it could lead to a takeover (good news) or an obstacle for the company management (bad news).

### Share buyback

When a company uses its profits to buy back their shares. This reduces the number of outstanding shares and makes the company ratios look healthier.

### Short Selling

The process where investors think the stock price of a company will go down, so they sell shares they don't own at a high price, hoping to buy them back at a later date at a lower price. Short sellers need to pay fees to borrow the shares that they don't own whilst they hold their short position.

### Tangible Assets

Assets that belong to a company that you can physically touch, see and feel. For example a retail company will own shops, land, trucks, stock etc. These assets are called Tangible Assets because they are physical and you can touch them.

### Turnover

The total amount of money taken by a company

during a set period of time.

## *Volume*

How many shares a company trades in a day. If the company trades significantly more than usual on a particular day, it can be described as a high-volume day. Important to take note is if there is a big price move on a high volume day as there is something real going on. If there is a big price move on a low volume day, it could just be a single aggressive buyer or seller moving the price. See also Market Maker and Liquidity.

# Index

## W

## Y